Guiding Light

NAVIGATING AUTISM WITH EMPATHY AND EXPERTISE

KASSANDRA ALVAREZ

ISBN: 979-8-89316-617-0 - eBook
ISBN: 979-8-89316-618-7 - Paperback
ISBN: 979-8-89316-619-4 - Hardcover

To every family navigating the ups and downs of supporting a child with autism—your strength, patience, and love are truly inspiring.

And to the incredible kids who remind us daily of the joy in every step forward, however small.

This book is for you.

Contents

Preface. vii

Introduction ix

Chapter 1: Your Life Does Not End At A Diagnosis xiii

Chapter 2: The "Why" Behind the Behavior" 13

Chapter 3: Mastering Responses to Challenging Behavior 17

Chapter 4: Maximizing Behavior with Reinforcement. 30

Chapter 5: The Impact and Use of Punishment in
           Behavior Management 38

Chapter 6: Influencing Behavior Before It Begins:
           Antecedent Interventions 46

Chapter 7: Navigating Transitions with Ease 53

Chapter 8: Empower & Enhance Communication Skills 62

Chapter 9: Embarking on the Potty Training Journey 75

Chapter 10: Tailoring Education to Your Child's Needs 80

Chapter 11: Creating Peaceful Bedtime Routines 86

Chapter 12: Optimizing Mealtimes and Feeding Experiences . . 91

Chapter 13: Embracing and Celebrating Your Child's
        Uniqueness 97

Preface

When I first started working with children with autism, I was amazed by both the unique challenges and the incredible joys that come with supporting these wonderful kids and their families. Over the years, I've seen how personalized strategies and a whole lot of heart can make a real difference. That's why I'm excited to share this book with you—Guiding Light: Navigating Autism with Empathy and Expertise.

This book is born from my passion for helping parents like you navigate the ups and downs of raising a child with autism. I know that every family's journey is different, filled with its own set of challenges and triumphs. My goal here is to provide you with practical, down-to-earth advice that's not just based on research, but also on real-life experiences.

You'll find tips and strategies to help with everything from communication to daily routines. I hope these pages give you the tools and encouragement you need to create a supportive and loving environment for your child.

A big thank you to the families and kids who have taught me so much along the way—you've really shaped my approach and kept me inspired. And of course, I'm grateful to my colleagues, mentors, and loved ones for their support and encouragement.

As you read through this book, I hope you feel supported and understood. The journey might have its challenges, but it's also filled with moments of connection and joy. Let's explore together how we can find peace and happiness in the amazing journey of parenting a child with autism.

Warmly,
Kassandra

Introduction

Receiving an autism diagnosis for your child can be a life-altering moment. The whirlwind of emotions—shock, confusion, fear, and even relief—can be overwhelming. Many parents find themselves asking,

"What does this mean for my child's future?"

"Will my child ever be able to live without me?"

"Will my child ever be able to talk?"

"Will my child's autism ever go away?"

"What caused my child to have autism?"

I understand the emotional complexities that often accompany a diagnosis. The feeling of relief because "you knew something was different," or because "my doctor didn't believe me and they told me that I needed to wait more time before having them tested." It can bring a wave of mixed emotions that might feel overwhelming at times. It's completely normal to experience a range of feelings, from shock and denial to grief and acceptance, as you navigate this new reality. You might find yourself grappling with anxiety and stress, worrying about your child's future and how to manage daily challenges.

This book is crafted to help you find clarity in these moments of uncertainty.

This book is not just about strategies; it's a testament to the power of compassion, knowledge, and the unwavering belief that every child possesses immense potential. Throughout these chapters, I will share evidence-based strategies that can help you foster your child's development. These include techniques to enhance communication skills, improve social interactions, and manage challenging behaviors.

My name is Kassandra, and I am a passionate advocate for children with autism and their families. Welcome to a journey that holds deep personal significance for me. As a dedicated Board-Certified Behavior Analyst (BCBA), my expertise is finely honed to cater to the unique needs of children on the autism spectrum. However, my true passion lies in guiding and empowering parents as they navigate the often intricate and overwhelming world of autism following their child's diagnosis.

As a BCBA, I have had the privilege of working with numerous families, each unique in their experiences and challenges. Through my professional journey, I have seen firsthand the transformative power of early intervention, consistent support, and most importantly, the unwavering love and dedication of parents. My work has reinforced my belief that parents are their child's greatest advocates and most important teachers.

If you don't advocate for your child with autism or provide the necessary support, they may face significant challenges that can impact their overall development and well-being. Without proper intervention, they may struggle to communicate effectively, manage their emotions, and navigate social situations, leading to increased frustration, isolation, and potential behavioral issues. Lack of support can also limit their access to educational opportunities tailored to their needs, hindering their ability to reach their full potential. Over time, this can result in lower self-esteem, reduced independence, and a diminished quality of life, making it essential to actively seek out and provide the appropriate resources, therapies, and advocacy they need to thrive. By taking the time to read this book and apply the strategies within, you are taking a powerful step in supporting your child.

One of the key strategies I advocate for in this book is the use of Applied Behavior Analysis (ABA). ABA is a science-based approach that uses techniques and principles to bring about meaningful and positive changes in behavior. I will guide you through the fundamentals of ABA, showing you how to apply these techniques in everyday situations to support your child's growth.

Creating an inclusive environment where your child feels safe, supported, and valued is crucial for their development. This involves not only adapting your home environment but also working with schools and community programs to ensure they are accommodating and supportive of your child's needs.

In the chapters that follow, we will discuss practical ways to make your home autism-friendly, collaborate with educators to create effective Individualized Education Programs (IEPs), and find community resources that offer additional support. Inclusion is about more than just physical spaces; it's about fostering a sense of belonging and acceptance in every aspect of your child's life.

It's also common to feel isolated, especially if others around you don't fully understand your journey. The emotional roller-coaster of celebrating your child's milestones while facing setbacks can be incredibly taxing, and the constant need to advocate for your child's needs might lead to advocacy fatigue.

This book is a comprehensive resource meticulously crafted to offer parents more than just answers. Through these pages, I hope to provide you with an insightful glimpse into your child's world, equipping you with the tools to foster growth, communication, and an unbreakable bond.

My goal is to empower you to advocate for your child's needs, navigate complex systems, and create an environment where your child can flourish. We will explore ways to build resilience and maintain hope, even in the face of challenges. You're not alone, and reaching out for help is a crucial step in caring for both your child and yourself.

Together, we will illuminate a path that leads to understanding, acceptance, and boundless love.

Join me as I walk you through the intricate journey of parenting a child with autism. Together, we will navigate the challenges, celebrate the triumphs, and build a future filled with hope and potential.

This journey is not just about managing a diagnosis; it's about embracing the unique strengths and capabilities of your child to empower them to reach their fullest potential.

CHAPTER 1

Your Life Does Not End At A Diagnosis

The day your child was diagnosed with autism may have been the day you felt like a part of you died inside, like you failed, or like you did something to your child that caused them to have been diagnosed. I want to be one of the people that will tell you that you did nothing wrong. I started working directly with diagnostics about 2 years after I became certified. It provided a new perspective, but it wasn't until I began working more closely with families while diagnosing in 2023 that everything changed for me. Two out of three families I spoke to "just knew." The diagnosis provided some sort of relief for them and even though they didn't know what was going to be of their life moving forward, they were thankful for it because they "just knew."

It was then that I realized that parents and families need my support too.

Every day, you are doing the very best that you know how and you are doing a great job at it. I say this and I want to reassure you of it, as I will throughout this book. There will be instances where you will get curious and you will likely search the internet. On the internet there will be blogs, newsletters, and even websites dedicated to telling you that you failed your child. I want to be the one to tell you that you did not. Your child having a diagnosis does not mean that you failed them. Your child having a diagnosis of autism means that your child may learn and do things a bit differently—and that's all.

As time goes on, there will be events in your child's life that may increase your awareness of your child's symptoms of autism. Events such as a family member coming over for the first time, traveling with them for the first time, their vaccine appointments, doctor appointments, and many other events that occur in the very early stages of your child's life. The symptoms of autism that you are now aware of may have been happening before, but the event that took place, from what I experience with talking to families, increased their awareness of the symptoms of autism. In some cases, it may cause them to believe that exposing them to a specific event is what caused their autism.

I talk about symptoms of autism, but what does that really mean and what do they look like? Symptoms of autism are those signs that you see in your child while they are developing that can be of concern for you—ones that indicate something may be wrong. A symptom of autism, or a sign of autism, looks different in every child, and I want to note that your child exhibiting any of what I will talk about does not mean that your child does or does not have autism. If you are concerned or would like to rule it out, please see your primary care doctor, and they can refer you to someone who can complete a diagnostic assessment.

When you became a parent, especially for the first time, you looked forward to your child's milestones. There are so many firsts to anticipate—at one to three months, your baby might start smiling at you, at four to six months, they might laugh for the first time, and at seven to nine months, they might start making a lot of different sounds. But what happens if these milestones don't come? What if you begin to notice they aren't meeting any of the typical milestones? This, along with other signs—like lining toys up, holding onto a toy but not playing with it, using a toy or object as a comfort item, struggling with change, or having difficulty with transitions—can be an early sign of autism. Repetitive behaviors, like hand-flapping when watching something exciting, whether it's a video on YouTube or a child going down a slide at the park, might also become noticeable. Another common sign is a need for routine—insisting on following the same daily pattern and becoming upset when it's disrupted. Some of the earliest signs can include a lack of eye contact or challenges with communication.

During regular check ups with your child and their primary care doctor, if concerns are noted, a comprehensive evaluation by specialists such as psychologists, neurologists, and speech therapists is conducted. Standardized tools like the Autism Diagnostic Observation Schedule (ADOS) and the Autism Diagnostic Interview-Revised (ADI-R) assess communication, social interaction, and behavior. Observations from parents and teachers are also considered. Once all assessments and interviews are conducted, your child is now diagnosed with autism. What happens next? Many times we go straight into, "How can I help them?" While there is nothing wrong in that being your next first step, and caring for a child with autism is important, taking care of *you* is even more important. If you don't take care of you, who is going to do it? Your life did not end when your child received that diagnosis. Your life instead, has been enhanced by a unique person who sees and does things differently, and that's so beautiful.

What are some things that you have done for you since your child received that diagnosis? Do you still get that monthly massage? Do you still take yourself out on dates? Do you make time to spend with your friends and loved ones? Do you and your partner still go out on that weekly date that you used to look forward to? Do you still make time to read? Do you look in the mirror and love what you see?

Prioritizing self-care is crucial for parents caring for a child with autism. Taking care of yourself not only enables you to better support your child and maintain your own well-being, but it also helps reduce stress and allows you to be more resilient and present for your child. When you take care of yourself, you provide a model and positive example for your child by teaching them how important it is to practice self-care and well being. Practicing self-care replenishes your energy levels, allowing you to tackle daily tasks with a greater sense of vitality.

A big question I ask my families during the intake process is, "What do you do to take care of you?"

One time, I asked this of a magnificent mother of three, and with tears in her eyes she said, "Nothing." Imagine how much more present and how much more joy you would feel if you took the time to prioritize you.

My role as a BCBA is to not only help your child, but also to provide a support system to you and your family. This, for me, is one of the most important parts of what I do. When a mom tells me that they took themselves on a shopping date or that a couple went out on a date since their child received their diagnosis, it truly makes my heart so full. Parents are superheroes and you truly deserve to take care of yourself. Navigating this diagnosis is probably not something you considered or planned for. It's new territory that you, as parents, have to navigate. I don't want you to ever feel like you're doing this alone. Figuring out how to help your child, or agreeing with a partner on things like discipline, can feel overwhelming and sometimes even lead to disagreements. As much as I want to prevent that stress, I'm here as a support system to help you navigate through it together.

As a parent, you're doing your best to navigate this unfamiliar journey, but it's not always easy, especially when stress and emotions run high. That's where I come in—to support you and help make things feel less overwhelming. Because we only know what we know.

If we were raised in a family where our parental figures resolved arguments with physical or vocal violence, we tend to do the same with the people around us. It's what we know. It's through active awareness of what we are doing that we can reprogram the subconscious to respond differently when we feel triggered.

For example, when I go into a home and notice that the parents or caregivers aren't on the same page about how to discipline their child or what the consequences should be, I step in and give them some homework. I ask them to work together on figuring out terms for grounding—like what they'll take away and what extra responsibilities their child will have. I do this so they can both feel good about what discipline looks like and, more importantly, so that their response comes from a place of love and not just reacting in the moment when their child does something they weren't ready for.

I help parents, like you, gain your power back and help you feel confident and good about the decisions you make with your child.

When you don't practice self care, you're more at risk of behaving or reacting in a way that can make your child's symptoms worse. Taking care of yourself then allows you to address challenges from a more reasonable mindset.

My challenge to you is to make yourself a priority. Start small; start with one thing a week and increase it to two things once you have made that one thing a part of your daily or weekly routine. Every month, carve out a day in your calendar to make it all about you. Don't feel guilty for doing this. You deserve every single second to yourself. Ask for help. There is someone out there who will be more than happy to take care of your child so you can spend the day doing as you want.

I have created a list of items that includes self-care strategies, managing stress and burnout, and balancing family life for you to use as a guide or a checklist for the rest of your life. It can help you with creating a self-care regime you can program into your life to put yourself first and begin the process of taking care of you.

By implementing these strategies, you can establish a harmonious family life that accommodates the needs of your child with autism while fostering open communication, realistic expectations, and a sense of joy and connection among all family members. This balance contributes to a nurturing and supportive environment for everyone in the family.

My heart in what I do is with my parents that I serve. When you take care of yourself and put yourself first, you are then better able to pour into the people you love even more.

a. Prioritizing Self-Care

Self-care isn't just a luxury—it's a necessity. Let's explore why self-care is vital and how you can incorporate it into your daily life:

Why Self-Care Matters:

- **Boost Your Well-Being:** Prioritizing self-care enhances your physical, emotional, and mental health, making you more resilient and present for your child.

- **Reduce Stress:** Engaging in self-care activities helps to alleviate stress, anxiety, and burnout, allowing you to navigate challenges with greater ease.

- **Be a Role Model:** Demonstrating self-care to your child teaches them the importance of looking after their own well-being.

- **Strengthen Relationships:** When you take care of yourself, you're better equipped to nurture healthy relationships with your child and others.

- **Replenish Your Energy:** Regular self-care recharges your energy levels, giving you the vitality needed to tackle daily tasks.

Practical Self-Care Strategies:

- **Stay Active:** Incorporate regular exercise to boost your mood, reduce stress, and improve your overall health.

- **Practice Mindfulness:** Engage in mindfulness or deep breathing exercises to help you stay present and manage stress effectively.

- **Pursue Hobbies:** Dedicate time to activities you love— whether it's reading, painting, gardening, or playing an instrument—to nurture your passions.

- **Connect Socially:** Maintain relationships with friends, family, or support groups to combat isolation and receive emotional support.

- **Eat Well:** A balanced diet fuels your body and mind, promoting overall wellness.

- **Prioritize Sleep:** Ensure you get enough sleep to support cognitive function and emotional resilience.

- **Express Creativity:** Explore creative outlets like journaling, crafting, or writing to express yourself and relieve stress.

- **Enjoy Nature:** Spend time outdoors, take nature walks, or simply relax in a natural setting to rejuvenate your mind.

- **Take Breaks:** Utilize respite care from trusted individuals or services to take short breaks and recharge.

The Power of Professional Support:

- **Alleviate Stress:** Therapy provides a safe space to discuss challenges, reducing parental stress and preventing burnout.

- **Develop Coping Strategies:** Therapists can equip you with tools to manage stress, emotions, and daily difficulties.

- **Foster Emotional Health:** Therapy allows for emotional expression, helping you to process feelings and improve your overall well-being.

- **Enhance Problem-Solving:** Gain effective problem-solving skills to navigate parenting challenges with confidence.

- **Improve Communication:** Strengthen your communication skills to better interact with your child and advocate for their needs.

- **Shift Your Mindset:** Therapy can help you reframe negative thoughts, fostering a more positive outlook.

- **Set Boundaries:** Learn how to balance responsibilities and prioritize self-care without feeling guilty.

- **Strengthen Parent-Child Relationships:** Work on parent-child dynamics with guidance from a therapist to foster a healthy, supportive relationship.

Remember, by prioritizing your self-care, you're not just benefiting yourself—you're also enhancing your ability to provide the best care for your child.

b. Managing Stress and Burnout

Adopting effective coping strategies and stress management techniques is essential to maintain your well-being. Here's how to incorporate these techniques into your routine:

Stress-Busting Techniques:

- **Deep Breathing:** Practice deep breathing. Inhale slowly through your nose, hold, and exhale through your mouth. Repeat to feel more centered.

- **Relaxation Exercises:** Try progressive muscle relaxation— tense and release each muscle group, moving from your toes to your head, to promote relaxation.

- **Mindfulness Meditation:** Dedicate a few minutes each day to mindfulness. Focus on your breath, letting go of judgments to stay calm and present.

- **Time Management:** Create a daily schedule, break tasks into manageable steps, and set aside time for self-care to avoid feeling overwhelmed.

- **Social Support:** Reach out to friends, family, or support groups. Sharing your experiences with others who under- stand can provide significant relief.

- **Journaling:** Writing down your thoughts and challenges helps you process emotions and gain clarity.

- **Set Healthy Boundaries:** Learn to say no when necessary and manage your time and energy effectively.

- **Use Positive Affirmations:** Replace negative thoughts with positive affirmations to boost confidence and self-esteem.

- **Practice Problem-Solving:** Break down challenges into smaller parts, brainstorm solutions, and take action. This proactive approach reduces stress.

Recognizing and Addressing Burnout:

- **Physical Signs:** Look out for fatigue, headaches, muscle tension, and sleep disturbances.

- **Emotional Symptoms:** Be aware of irritability, mood swings, feelings of helplessness, and increased sensitivity.

- **Cognitive Struggles:** Watch for difficulty concentrating, memory issues, and constant worry.

- **Behavioral Changes:** Notice any tendencies to isolate yourself, withdraw from activities, or neglect self-care.

Implementing Self-Care Practices:

- **Prioritize Your Well-Being:** Make self-care a daily priority, not just an afterthought.

- **Delegate Responsibilities:** Share the load with family, friends, or professionals to ease your burden.

- **Set Realistic Goals:** Focus on what's achievable, not perfection.

- **Take Regular Breaks:** Even short breaks can recharge your energy.

- **Engage in Enjoyable Activities:** Pursue hobbies, exercise, or relaxation techniques that bring you joy.

- **Seek Professional Help:** Don't hesitate to consult a therapist or counselor when stress becomes overwhelming.

- **Spend Quality Family Time:** Engage in enjoyable activities with your child to strengthen your bond.

By integrating these strategies, you can manage stress and prevent burnout, ensuring that you remain healthy, focused, and capable of providing the best care for your child.

c. Balancing Family Life

Juggling the needs of your child while maintaining a harmonious family life can be challenging, but it's achievable with effective time management and prioritization.

Creating Balance:

- **Daily Routines:** Develop a daily schedule that balances routines, therapy, school, and family time, providing structure and predictability.

- **Prioritize Wisely:** Identify essential tasks and prioritize them based on importance and urgency.

- **Time Blocks:** Allocate specific time blocks for work, self-care, and family activities to ensure that all areas are addressed.

- **Flexible Routines:** Create routines that can adapt to unexpected changes while maintaining a sense of stability.

- **Family Meetings:** Regularly hold family meetings to discuss schedules, responsibilities, and any necessary adjustments.

- **Delegate Tasks:** Share responsibilities among family members to lighten the load and foster teamwork.

- **Shared Calendar:** Use a digital calendar that all family members can access to stay informed about upcoming events and commitments.

- **Personal Time:** Schedule regular breaks for each family member to pursue individual interests and self-care.

Emphasizing Communication, Realistic Expectations, and Joy:

- **Open Communication:** Foster clear communication to ensure understanding and unity within the family. Discuss challenges, needs, and expectations openly.

- **Set Realistic Goals:** Avoid unrealistic pressures by setting achievable goals, which promote a sense of accomplishment.

- **Define Roles:** Clearly define each family member's caregiving role to promote a sense of teamwork and shared responsibility.

- **Adaptability:** Stay flexible and be prepared to adapt plans based on your child's needs and circumstances.

- **Find Joy in Daily Life:** Look for moments of joy and connection within your daily routines. These moments reinforce positive experiences and strengthen family bonds.

- **Celebrate Achievements:** Acknowledge and celebrate each family member's achievements, no matter how small. This fosters a sense of pride and accomplishment.

- **Quality Family Time:** Make time for activities that everyone enjoys, creating opportunities for bonding and relaxation.

- **Shared Activities:** Engage in activities that promote togetherness, such as family games, outings, or shared hobbies.

- **Build Resilience:** Embrace challenges as opportunities for growth, helping to build resilience within the family.

- **Establish a Support Network:** Surround yourself with a network of friends, extended family, and support groups to provide emotional support and practical assistance.

- **Focus on Progress:** Celebrate your child's progress and milestones, no matter how small. This positive focus helps maintain a healthy perspective.

Visit **www.promptpathconsulting.
com/resources** to find the self-care
journal I crafted with love, just for you.

My goal for you is to learn how to take care of you so
that you can then implement all that I am about to teach you.

In this, *"ABA therapy in a book,"* as I am calling it, there will be
examples, personal scenarios, and different skills that you can use
to teach your child. I have worked with hundreds of families, but
the number of families out there that still need access to ABA is
even more significant. This book is for you, a parent or caregiver
of a person with an intellectual disability or behavioral challenges.
This book was created using the science of Applied Behavior
Analysis to support you when you can't work directly with someone
like me, or even if you have and just need a quick reminder. I hope
to teach you everything that I know has helped my clients so you
are able to help your child.

To every parent out there, I see you.

In the following chapters, you'll find a section called 'ABA At Home In Action.' These are designed to bring the concepts we've discussed to life with practical, step-by-step strategies you can use right at home. Think of these sections as your go-to guide for applying what you've learned and making ABA techniques work for you and your child.

CHAPTER 2

The "Why" Behind the Behavior"

Before I became a BCBA, I was an RBT—a therapist under the supervision of a BCBA. When the covid pandemic started, I transitioned from an in-clinic RBT to an in-home RBT. I had never been in the home before, but after that experience, I realized that we are so needed in the home, sometimes more than in the clinic. I was working with one family and my client was a school-aged child. My client and I had worked together in the center, but in the home, parents had told us that they hit their head against hard surfaces a lot and that they also threw a lot of tantrums. Even though it's sad to hear this, this is the reality of working with a child with autism.

Throughout our time together, we made a lot of progress. I taught my client how to talk using more than one word, we worked on labeling and conversation skills, amongst other things. Now, before I finish the rest of this story, I will say, as a therapist, I realized early on that children are children. They will listen to some people and others, they will not. This could be for a number of reasons, but the main one that I see now is instructional control.

Instructional control was a key piece of that progress. Having instructional control means that an individual consistently responds to and complies with instructions or commands given by you. Instructional control is essential, especially when you are teaching a new skill or managing the child's behavior. This not only applies to children with autism, but to all people.

When you have instructional control with a child, this means that the child will follow your instruction or do as you tell them to, most of the time. When you don't have any instructional control with a child, the child will likely engage in unwanted behavior any time you ask them to do something or simply not do as you tell them to.

As the time passed and I worked more and more with my client, I was able to establish great instructional control. This was done by playing with them, being kind to them, and overall having them trust me and want to be with me. I followed a lot of their lead, especially in the very beginning of getting to know them and placed very little demands. I did this because I wanted them to want to be with me. If I had gone into the sessions and immediately started placing instructions, the likelihood of them listening to me over time was going to be very low.

Over time, they listened to me more than they did to anyone else, including their parents. When I would leave the home of my client, the next day their parents would tell me about how they did after I left and every time they said the same thing; either they would have a tantrum, yell, or just flat out not listen. This happened often and it did not make any sense to me considering that when I was there, they behaved well and we got a lot done.

I don't want to say that I did not believe the family, but it did not seem real that my client would completely regress when I left.

One day though, I was leaving their home and mom shouted out to me, "*Kassandra, look!*" I looked and there they were, grabbing something they knew they should not be touching. But the even more bizarre thing is that as soon as I looked at them, they stopped. Yes, I did have great instructional control with this client, but there was more going on as well.

Throughout my entire experience in the world of applied behavior analysis, one of the most important things that I learned is that there are four functions of behavior. These are sensory stimulation, escape/avoidance, attention, and tangibles. A behavior maintained by the function of sensory stimulation is when individuals engage in certain behaviors because they find them stimulating or satisfying in some sensory way. For example, someone might repeatedly tap their foot because they enjoy the sensation it provides.

This is different from behavior maintained by the function of escape/avoidance, which looks like engaging in a behavior to escape or avoid an unpleasant situation, task, or item. For instance, a student might engage in disruptive behavior in class to avoid doing challenging tasks or to escape from the teacher's instructions.

A behavior maintained by attention includes doing something in order to get attention from a single person or a group of people. This attention could be positive or negative. An example for seeking negative attention is when a child acts out to get attention from parents or peers, even if it's in the form of reprimands or scolding. Positive attention, however, is asking their dad, in an appropriate way, to play with them.

Finally, behavior maintained by tangibles looks like doing something to obtain tangible rewards or access to an item. This could include things like food, toys, money, or other items of value. For instance, a child might complete their chores to access their phone or additional screentime.

For each human being, the behavior will look different, but the functions are all the same. This does not only apply to children with autism or only to children, by the way. We all do things for a reason, at all stages of our life, whether that be because it feels good to us, because we want attention, because we want to get out of something, or because we want to earn something for completing something.

In the example with my client, yes, I had excellent instructional control, but their behavior was also maintained by one or several of the functions.

As a behavior analyst, part of my job is to educate and train parents. I think of this as the most important part of the job because, without parents knowing what we are teaching their child and why we are teaching these things, your child may make progress while they are with me, but they may revert to being the same child you always knew when I leave.

In the following chapter, I will go into detail about each function of behavior so that maybe you can identify and even be able to help your child based on the information I am about to share with you.

Get some real-world tips on gaining instructional control with our guide—head over to **www.promptpathconsulting.com/ resources** to download it and start using these strategies with your child.

CHAPTER 3

Mastering Responses to Challenging Behavior

N ow that we have talked a bit about the functions of behavior, we can talk about what all of that means. When we respond to behavior according to its function, we are either going to cause it to increase or decrease. A behavior increasing or decreasing can be good or bad depending on what the behavior is. A behavior increasing or decreasing is also dependent on the person or people that are around that behavior. For children, these people would be their caregivers.

For example, in children, head banging overall is a behavior we want to see decrease and I am not sure that anyone would argue against that. Procrastination, however, could be a behavior that some people may want to decrease, but to other people, it may not affect them. This is individualized, as every single person on this earth is different.

Let's get into the functions!

Attention

Providing attention to a behavior that is maintained by attention will cause for the behavior to either increase or decrease. Something really important to note here is that there is positive and negative attention-seeking.

Positive attention seeking can look like your child calling out for you by saying, "Mom." It can also look like your child patting you on the leg to be able to get your attention. Lastly, for some more advanced learners, it can look like your child saying, "Excuse me," to be able to get your attention. It is called positive attention seeking because they are engaging in a desirable behavior to be able to get your attention.

Negative attention seeking can look like a child acting out and having a tantrum to get attention from parents or peers. For example, your child is throwing something at the wall, hitting their sibling, or even yelling because they want you to pay attention to them. These can all be examples of negative attention seeking, because they are engaging in a behavior that is not desirable to get some sort of attention from you.

There are many behaviors that can be maintained by attention in a negative way. For example, let's say a child wants you to play with them, and instead of asking you for what they want, they scream and throw themselves on the floor because they know that it causes you to give them some sort of attention, including telling them to "stop." This form of attention seeking would be called negative attention seeking.

An appropriate form to seek attention in this example would have been the child asking for the parent to play with them, tapping them on a part of their body, or even pointing to the toy they wanted their parent to play with them with.

What I always tell my families is that when you notice a behavior may be maintained by attention, the best thing you can do is not give it any attention—for now. The reason is that even one instance of giving your child attention during a negative, attention-seeking behavior can make it happen again and again.

You might be wondering what some forms of attention are. High-fives, hugs, reprimands, talking, and even eye contact are all forms of attention you might give, whether for positive or negative attention-seeking behaviors

Sometimes kids with autism might actually go after negative attention instead of positive attention, and there are a few reasons behind that. For starters, they might not really get the difference between the two types of attention. If a certain behavior always gets a reaction, they'll probably stick with it, even if it's negative. Communication challenges can make things tougher too—if they can't easily say what they need, frustration can show up as negative behaviors. The thing is, the response they get from adults when they act out might be more predictable and immediate than when they do something positive, which can feel less consistent. Sensory sensitivities also come into play. Sometimes acting out is their way of coping with feeling overwhelmed. And for some kids, positive reinforcement doesn't always click because they don't fully understand how their behavior leads to a reward. When you mix in challenges with emotional regulation, frustration and anxiety can drive those negative behaviors even more. And if adults aren't consistent with rewarding positive actions but always react to the negative ones, it makes sense why the child might turn to negative behaviors to get that guaranteed response.

What can we do if we are not sure if the child is seeking positive or negative attention? This is individualized to the parent. Every parent parents a different way and what is an appropriate way to seek attention to one parent may not look the same to another.

I personally would say that asking for something, typically, is an overall good way to seek some form of attention. For example, you can have your child ask for something using their words. If they don't have words, you can teach them to use icons or an AAC device to communicate with you. In addition to these two ways of communication, you can also have them point, tap you, or communicate in the way they may that is appropriate as long as it does not involve them acting out to get your attention. If they don't know how to ask for something in the very early stages of talking, you are also able to talk for them. What I mean is for you to vocally have them repeat whatever it is that you want them to say. Talking for your child so that they can repeat what you want for them to say is okay, especially when they are learning something for the first time. When your child is learning to ask for attention in an appropriate way, when in the past they only knew to yell and throw themselves on the ground, they will not know how to use their words and therefore, it is something that will have to be taught.

Escape

A behavior maintained by the function of escape may look like a person doing something so that they can get out of doing another thing. Escape maintained behaviors can look like procrastination, asking to leave when assigned a task, or getting up to use the bathroom when assigned a task. I have also seen children cry when they are told to take a shower and pretend that they are sick while at school so that they can be sent home.

One of my favorite examples for an escape maintained behavior with one of my kiddos was when they were asked to sit at the table, they would say they were thirsty and ask to go get water every time. This was one that took some time to catch on to, and the way we did it was because every day, the time it took them to get water was extended and in some cases, they would even ask to go to the bathroom as well.

One day, my therapist mentioned it to me, so what we did to see if it was an escape maintained behavior is have water ready for them and make sure that they used the bathroom before any sort of task was presented. We then asked them to come sit, and as we expected, they began to complain and cry out that they did not want to work. This confirmed the function. I will say, over time, the crying and complaining got better. We stuck with the plan and eventually, they completed the task and all was fine.

Like any other behavior, though, it looks different in everyone. The biggest thing that you can look for is how the child or person responds when you either give in to their behavior or as soon as they stop doing what they were supposed to be doing.

For example, when you tell your child to go brush their teeth, they start crying, maybe even without tears, and you tell them that it's okay and they can wait a few minutes before going. When you do this, do they immediately stop crying and are fine? If the answer is yes, the behavior is likely maintained by escape.

To simplify what happened in this scenario:

1. You asked them to do something they maybe didn't want to do
2. They started to cry
3. You told them they didn't have to do it right now.

Because this is the response that took place, there is a high chance of the child crying when asked to do something they don't want to in the future. It takes one time of us giving in to the function of a behavior for that behavior to continue to occur time and time again.

Some ways in which you can replace some of their behaviors that are escape maintained can look like seeking or finding out what it is they want to do or maybe even the reason they don't want to do what you asked them to do. When you find these things out, you are able to use them as reinforcers or as a reward for the completion of the task they didn't want to do in the first place.

Let's say the reason they don't want to complete the task is that it is a non-preferred task. For this specific example, a Nintendo Switch is their highest reinforcer. In ABA, we use what is called the Premack principle, which means 'first-then.' For this, you would have them complete their non-preferred task first, and then they could have their reinforcer, or Nintendo Switch. If they were already playing with it at the time that you asked them to complete the task, you could offer them more time, or maybe even something more creative. Again, what you offer them does not have to be forever. Once they start to respond consistently in the way you want them to, you can start to fade out the reinforcer, and in no time, if you remain consistent, they may not need a reward to complete the task.

The most important thing to keep in mind when doing all of this is that you have to present the reinforcer, the Nintendo Switch, before you ask them to do something that they don't want to. For example, "Hey Jeff, what is it that you want to play with?" and in this specific example with the Nintendo Switch you tell Jeff, "Okay, first let's go brush your teeth and then you can have your Nintendo Switch."

What you are doing in the specific example is you are offering them a reinforcer for completing something they didn't want to do. Offering a person or a child a reward—especially in the very beginning when you notice they're doing a lot of things that aren't in anyone's best interest—when asking them to complete some of their least favorite things is not a bad thing. I also want you to know that it is okay to do this because rewards, despite being something you might have to use a lot of in the very beginning, won't have to be used forever.

In a different example, one thing that you can do is offer them choices of things that they may want to do or have. Let's say they love their Nintendo Switch, but maybe they also love M&Ms. What you can do for this example is ask them, 'Do you want M&Ms or do you want to play with your Nintendo Switch?' Once they answer, you can use whatever it is they said and tell them, 'First we are going to go brush your teeth, and then you can have ___.'

Another way that you can replace behavior that is escape-maintained is to have them ask for breaks. As a BCBA, breaks are something that I do utilize, especially for older kids. When I am teaching a child or anyone anything, I always put myself in the shoes of the person. For example, if I am asked or need to complete a task that I know I don't want to do, I know that taking breaks will allow me to step away from it and ultimately lead to me being more productive. I will always allow a child that I am working with to take a break, if and when they ask for it—the key word being 'ask.' If they don't know how to ask, I will teach them how to ask.

In therapy, where we spend a lot of one-on-one time with children, we sometimes use a tactic called 'following through' or 'waiting them out.' This means we'll patiently wait for however long it takes for the child to complete the task we've asked them to do. This approach is something I usually use only with children who already know how to do the task we're asking them to complete. For example, if a child is asked to clean up their toys and they know how to do it but are hesitating, we might just wait quietly until they start and finish the job. It helps reinforce that completing the task is what's expected, without putting too much pressure on them.

Now, I understand that this might not always be practical at home, where time can be tight and there are lots of other things going on. So while 'waiting them out' is a useful technique in therapy, it might not always fit into your daily routine. It's good to know about this approach, but at home, you might need to find other strategies that work better for your situation and your child's readiness. It's all about finding what helps best in your own environment.

Tangible / Access

A behavior maintained by this function means that we are engaging in a behavior because we are trying to get access to an item or an action. For example, with children, let's say your snack items are on the highest part of your pantry. Every time your child wants a snack, they cry at the pantry. The cry has a tangible function - they're crying because they want a snack. Another example of a behavior with tangible function is that a child might cry when a preferred item is removed and stop crying as soon as you give it back.

To decrease a behavior that has a tangible function, a good place to start is by teaching your child to ask for what they want. You can use the form of communication your child is comfortable with, and initially, you might even start by teaching them to point to the item they want. If your child can't have the item they're asking for, another skill to teach is waiting. For example, if your child has been crying for hours because you took something away or because they want access to an item, giving them the instruction, 'Wait,' can make all the difference and significantly reduce the amount of time they cry.

When teaching a child to wait, one thing to remember is to start small and not increase the amount of time quickly. At first, they may only be able to wait a few seconds, but over time, they may not even remember what it is that you took away and tolerate removing it altogether. My technique for waiting is to let them know that you are going to take it away. For example, tell them, 'My turn,' and then once you have removed it, tell them, 'Wait.' Once you have told them to wait, because every child is different, some will be okay with just a verbal reminder, but some may need a visual of something counting down or even the sound of an alarm when the waiting is over. You will know if your child needs more than just a verbal reminder when you have tried it multiple times and your child is still not able to wait. Trial and error is what will help you. Once the time they're waiting for is over, praise them with something like, 'Great job waiting,' and then give them back the item. You can do this as many times as you want during the day. The more times, the better. Once they are able to wait for the amount of time you started with for a few days, you can increase the time and continue to do this until you reach your goal.

Once your child is able to wait for the amount of the goal time, you are always able to work on telling your child "No" or "Not right now" or even offering an alternative such as, "You can't have this right now, but you can have ___." These different options will come with time and they may be here sooner than later if you stay consistent and work on it multiple times throughout your day.

Some children will learn to tolerate you removing something, telling them to wait, or denying them something really quickly and others will take months. No matter how long it is taking your child, keep going. One day, you will tell your child 'no' or 'wait,' and they will tolerate it, and it's going to be beautiful.

Automatic

This looks like a child or a person doing something because it feels good to them. A personal example of a behavior with an automatic function is when I was young; rocking myself felt good to me. The behavior of rocking served no purpose other than that it felt good to me.

For a child, and more specifically a child with autism, a behavior that has an automatic function can look like hand flapping, pacing, or rocking. Again they do this because it feels good to them, and they are getting some sort of sensory stimulation from it, that feels good to them. Some behaviors I have seen that have an automatic function in autism—and overall—can also be dangerous, such as hitting their head against the wall or hurting themselves in other ways. These behaviors, even though they can be dangerous, feel good to them despite potentially causing harm.

Behaviors that have an automatic function are so interesting because the way that I look at them is, unless they are interrupting their quality of life or a danger to self or others, I don't see why they need to be interrupted or decreased. I personally don't mess with them if they are still able to do the things that they need to in their day to day and if they are not interrupting their quality of life.

When I do need to interrupt them as a clinician is when the behavior is interrupting their quality of life or is a danger to themselves or others. The worst-case scenario with a dangerous behavior that has an automatic function is that they could end up dying because of a behavior that feels good to them. I am not going to give specific suggestions with specific examples of what you can do because it's going to look different with every person. What I will say is that with dangerous behavior, my suggestion to you is to do your best to find a replacement for them. You might need to block them, but you also might need to distract them from doing something that you don't want them to be doing. Distractions are super important in ABA. We call them redirection, and they are a way to get them out of what you don't want them to be doing.

When beginning to manage a behavior according to its function, remember: patience will be everything. You will have to stay strong, not attend to their past behavior, and doing this could potentially lead to the behavior getting worse before it gets better. But if you stay consistent and don't give in to their behavior the moment it gets hard, your child's behavior will increase or decrease and do what you want it to.

It's a marathon, not a sprint. Remember that, always.

ABA At Home In Action:

1. Attention-Seeking Behavior

- **Positive Reinforcement**: Provide attention for positive behaviors. Praise or reward your child when they display desirable actions.

- **Planned Ignoring**: Ignore minor inappropriate behaviors that are done to seek attention, as long as they are not harmful.

- **Structured Time**: Set aside specific times during the day for one-on-one attention, so your child knows they will have dedicated attention periods.

- **Teach Replacement Behaviors**: Teach your child appropriate ways to gain attention, such as using words or gestures.

2. Escape or Avoidance Behavior

- **Task Analysis**: Break tasks into smaller, manageable steps to make them less overwhelming.

- **Choice Offering**: Allow your child to have some control by offering choices within tasks.

- **First-Then Statements**: Use statements like "First do your homework, then you can play" to provide a clear structure.

- **Gradual Exposure**: Gradually increase the difficulty of tasks to build tolerance and reduce the urge to escape.

3. Access to Tangibles

- **Clear Rules**: Establish and communicate clear rules about when and how your child can access desired items.

- **Use of Token Systems**: Implement a token or reward system where your child earns tokens for positive behavior that can be exchanged for desired items.

- **Teach Delay of Gratification**: Practice waiting skills by gradually increasing the wait time before your child can access the desired item.

- **Structured Routines**: Incorporate the desired items into a routine schedule, so your child knows when they can expect to access them.

4. Sensory-Seeking Behavior

- **Provide Alternatives**: Offer appropriate sensory activities that fulfill your child's sensory needs, such as playing with a fidget toy or engaging in physical activity.

- **Sensory Breaks**: Schedule regular sensory breaks throughout the day to help your child self-regulate.

- **Create a Sensory-Friendly Environment**: Modify the home environment to reduce sensory overload or provide sensory-rich activities.

- **Teach Self-Regulation**: Help your child recognize when they need sensory input and teach them strategies to seek it appropriately.

General Strategies

- **Consistent Routine**: Maintain a predictable routine to provide structure and reduce anxiety.

- **Communication**: Enhance communication skills to help your child express their needs appropriately.

- **Positive Reinforcement**: Use positive reinforcement to encourage and sustain desired behaviors.

- **Modeling**: Demonstrate appropriate behavior for your child to imitate.

- **Monitoring and Adjusting**: Continuously monitor your child's behavior and adjust strategies as needed.

Discover the key to understanding your child's behavior with our downloadable workbook, 'Identifying the Function of Your Child's Behavior.' Access it now at **www.promptpathconsulting. com/resources**

CHAPTER 4

Maximizing Behavior with Reinforcement

L et's say your child just does something they typically don't do, maybe they are working on learning a new skill, or maybe you want to increase a certain behavior. When doing this, the first thing you might think to do is give your child a reward or to praise them in some sort of way. The reward or praise then causes for the behavior or skill to continue to happen and increase. This entire process is called reinforcement.

Reinforcement, defined, is the process of increasing the likelihood that a specific behavior will occur again in the future by delivering a reinforcer immediately after the behavior. In simple terms it means that you are adding or removing something to cause a behavior to increase.

To be more specific, there are two types of reinforcement: positive and negative reinforcement. Positive reinforcement means that you are adding something to cause a behavior to increase and negative reinforcement means that you are removing something to cause a behavior to increase.

Positive Reinforcement

Positive reinforcement is a tool that not only works for children with autism, but for any person. The main benefits of positive reinforcement are that it increases motivation by adding something desirable, provides clear feedback about the task, and enhances learning. An example of positive reinforcement is giving a child an edible reward for learning a new skill. The skill can be anything from going to the bathroom or saying their name when you ask them, "What is your name?" As human beings, food is naturally one of our higher reinforcers. If your child has autism, you might have already learned that this may not be the case with them. This is okay because you can use a device, a toy, praise, gestures, or anything else that they love.

A really big thing to know when using positive reinforcement is that the rewards you are using don't have to be forever. This applies to everything—food items or even telling them 'great job.' Just because you have to use it now does not mean you will have to use it forever. Positive reinforcement works in all stages of life and is something you can fade out or remove slowly as you notice that the skill is happening without using a reward. If the skill or the behavior you want to happen is happening every single time you ask the learner to do something, then the chances of you being able to fade out—or gradually stop giving—the reward are very high. A key thing you do not want to do is remove or fade out the reward too quickly. For example, let's say you notice that it has been two days and they're doing really well with the skills you are teaching them, and you think it might be a good opportunity to go ahead and completely remove all the rewards. If you do this, you could run into some challenging behavior when you don't give them a reward they were expecting, or you might see the skill not happening as frequently as you want.

When using reinforcement you will want to make sure that you are clear with a specific skill or behavior that you want to see increase. When delivering a reward you want to make sure that you do it immediately or as soon as they did what you asked them to do. If you delay the reinforcer, the chances of the learner knowing why you are providing them with a reward is very low.

For example, if you are trying to teach your child their name and you ask them, "What is your name?" and they respond correctly, in that very moment, as soon as they respond, the idea is that you will give them whatever it is that you said you would. In this same example, instead of giving the reward to them immediately, let's say you wait maybe an hour because you didn't have whatever you promised them handy. There is a high chance that your child will not remember why you are giving them a reward and they may just think that you are giving them something they like for a reason that is not what you initially wanted. Providing your child with a reward immediately lets them know in that moment that they did what you asked them to and that this is why you are giving them something. When you delay the reward or reinforcer, you are then giving them a snack if you are using an edible, or giving them their favorite toy, but in their minds, it's no longer a reinforcer for doing what you initially asked them to.

With reinforcement as well, you want to make sure that what you are offering is motivating to them, for them to keep doing what you want them to do. Something else to keep in mind is that if you are going to be using some of their favorite things, you will want to remove those things from their day to day. The reason for this is because if they are still using their Nintendo Switch, for example, every single day when they normally do, in their day-to-day, when you are trying to teach them something new, the Nintendo Switch won't be as motivating. This can be for many reasons, but the big one I believe is that children know what you are doing and they are very smart. Especially in the beginning, they pick up on how we do things. If they notice that you are still giving them their Nintendo Switch whenever you typically do, then whenever you ask them to do something new while using the Nintendo Switch as the reward, the chances of them learning the skill successfully are a lot lower because they know that you are still going to give them their Nintendo Switch like you normally do.

One thing I have learned in my career is that children know exactly what is going on. They are some of the smartest age groups I have ever met. As adults we don't typically think this because we are a lot older than them and they are only children, but they pick up on things so quickly and they know how to get what they want a lot of the time. Keep this in mind whenever you are doing something or whenever you respond in a way that maybe you are not proud of. Something I always tell parents is that it takes one time for us to respond in a certain way to reinforce the behavior that we may not want to see happening.

Negative Reinforcement

We have talked a little bit about positive reinforcement, so now let's talk about negative reinforcement. Negative reinforcement, defined, means that you are removing something that you don't want to do or removing something that they may not like to do, which will increase the chances of the behavior happening again in the future. In other words, this also means that you are taking something away so you can increase a behavior.

Negative reinforcement for me was always a lot more challenging to understand than positive reinforcement. I know for the parents I worked with, whenever I explained it to them, sometimes they didn't understand either. So what I'm going to do next is make it a little bit simpler and just give examples because I know that for me, examples work a lot better. At the end of the day, something to keep in mind is that every child is different and so what works for your child isn't what's going to work for every child.

An example of negative reinforcement that we all know of is the reminder in our cars telling us to buckle our seat belts. I have even been in cars where the music or radio completely turn off if you don't buckle your seatbelt within a certain time frame. Removing the sound that the seatbelt reminder makes or having our music not turn off reinforces the behavior of buckling our seatbelts, which therefore encourages us to buckle our seatbelts to avoid all of that from happening in the first place.

A good example if you have children that are in school for negative reinforcement is studying to avoid bad grades. Removing the possibility of getting a bad grade serves as negative reinforcement for studying. This just means that you are likely to study so that you won't get a bad grade and so that good grades increase.

Here is another example with children. Imagine your child really dislikes the feeling of their shoes being too tight. Every time they go to put them on, they get frustrated and want to take them off. So, to make it easier, you loosen the laces, and the discomfort goes away. Over time, the child learns that if they loosen their laces first, they avoid that uncomfortable feeling altogether. In this case, you're removing the discomfort (the tight shoes), which encourages them to put on their shoes in a way that's more comfortable for them. Every child is different, but it's all about figuring out what motivates your child to avoid something they find unpleasant.

I have two more examples for you, in the case it still is not too clear, and listen, I get it. The next example I will talk about is taking pain medication. Let's say you have a headache and you are not feeling well. Taking pain medication typically means that your headache will go away, right? Well, the relief that you got from taking the pain medication serves as a negative reinforcer because the next time you have a headache or any form of pain you are likely to take the pain medication again.

Hopefully, it is starting to make a little bit more sense. The last example, which is my favorite because it applies very much to my life, is the alarm clock in the morning, or when it is time to wake up. I don't like the way that they sound and I don't like the way that the sound makes me feel because if you're anything like me, my heart starts to race when I hear the alarm and it's just not a good feeling. Waking up and turning off the alarm to stop the sound that it is making reinforces the behavior of waking up. The next time that your alarm goes off you are likely to click the turn-off button as soon as possible and wake up instead of allowing your alarm to continue.

Understanding positive and negative reinforcement can help you guide your child's behavior in a positive way. Instead of reacting when they misbehave, you can focus on rewarding the behaviors we want to see more of. By using positive reinforcement, like praise and rewards, and occasionally using negative reinforcement to remove unpleasant tasks, you can help your child learn and grow in a supportive and encouraging environment.

ABA At Home In Action:

1. Identify Specific Behaviors to Reinforce

- **Be Clear and Specific**: Determine which positive behaviors you want to encourage (e.g., doing homework, sharing toys) and which negative behaviors you want to reduce (e.g., tantrums, hitting).

- **Communicate Expectations**: Clearly explain these behaviors to your child so they understand what is expected.

2. Choose Effective Reinforcers and Consequences (Consequences are what happens directly after a behavior, influencing whether the behavior will be repeated.)

- **Positive Reinforcers**: Identify rewards that your child finds motivating, such as praise, stickers, extra playtime, or a favorite treat.

- **Negative Reinforcers**: Identify ways to remove an aversive stimulus to increase desirable behaviors. For example, if a child completes a task, you might remove an undesired chore or a frustrating task to encourage the behavior.

3. Implement Immediate and Consistent Reinforcement

- **Immediate Feedback**: Provide positive reinforcement immediately after the desired behavior and apply negative reinforcement promptly after the negative behavior to strengthen the association.

- **Consistency is Key**: Apply reinforcement and consequences consistently each time the behavior occurs to establish clear expectations and build habits.

4. Use Specific and Constructive Feedback

- **Positive Feedback**: Be specific about what behavior you are praising (e.g., "Great job sharing your toys with your sister!").

- **Constructive Feedback**: When using negative reinforcement, clearly explain why the aversive stimulus is being removed and what behavior you expect instead (e.g., "Because you finished your homework, we are removing the extra chores for today. Keep up the good work with your tasks!").

5. Monitor Progress and Make Adjustments

- **Track Behavior**: Keep a record of your child's behavior to see which reinforcers and consequences are most effective and to ensure consistent application.

- **Adjust Strategies**: Be flexible and ready to adjust your reinforcement and consequence strategies based on what works best for your child's development and changing needs.

CHAPTER 5

The Impact and Use
of Punishment in
Behavior Management

P unishment and the field of ABA...I am a behavior analyst, and one thing that the field of ABA can be frowned upon for is because we use the word 'punishment.' Anytime there is any use of punishment in a child's treatment, most companies have a set of requirements, such as, it needs to go through a board or through multiple supervisors before it is used. Some companies don't use punishment all together, and this is something that is clearly stated in their handbook.

In ABA, punishment means adding or removing a stimulus (or thing) to decrease a behavior. Because we are human, we may see the word 'punishment' and automatically think of something bad, but that is based on our human experience and not on the field of ABA. Before I get into the chapter, my intention is to talk about punishment and help everyone who's reading this see it with an open mind. I'm going to talk about punishment in the way that I have used it in the past and in the way that I saw it work and help the children it's been used with. I'll provide definitions and examples of how I have used it, how it has worked, and also when I have used it and had to pivot.

Punishment is a tool that can really help families, if it is used the way it was intended to be used.

One experience that I recall very well was before I was a BCBA. A client that I worked with engaged in very loud vocalizations. These vocalizations were not your normal scream-every-once-in-a-while, they were high frequency and very, very loud. This client, specifically, did these vocalizations whenever they didn't want to do something and whenever they wanted to get out of doing something. At its very worst, it was happening over 100 times a day and one thing to keep in mind is that they were only with us for about six hours a day. One hundred times over six hours is a lot of screaming. Now, with behavior, if it was happening with us at therapy, it means that it's happening at home as well, sometimes more and sometimes less. This is not always the case, but in this case, it was happening at home and parents didn't know what else to do.

As behavior analysts, we're required to explore every possible form of reinforcement before even thinking about using punishment. This is part of our ethics code, and it's something we take very seriously. We try everything—praise, tangible rewards, activities the child enjoys—anything that could motivate positive behavior. Only after we've completely exhausted every reinforcement option, and done our homework by looking into all the scientific research that might help, do we consider punishment as a last resort. Punishment isn't something we jump to; it's a carefully thought-out decision made only when we've tried everything else first.

Before we could implement anything for this client, we needed the parents' approval. Once we had that, we moved on to assessments. These included testing out different forms of punishment to see which ones would effectively reduce the behavior. For instance, we might try adding exercise or giving a reprimand. Just to clarify, when we talk about punishment, we mean adding or removing something to decrease a behavior. After conducting a range of assessments, we found that a reprimand was the most effective in reducing the unwanted behavior. With this finding, we went back to the parents to get their approval for including this in the treatment plan. They agreed, and within a few days, we saw a significant drop in vocalizations—down to almost zero each day. This was a big improvement from the more than 100 screams a day we had been seeing before. Now, the child was only screaming up to five times a day, which was a huge win for us.

I talk about this because I know how much is said about ABA and the use of punishment and I want to provide clarity on how good it could be for you and your child, if it is needed. For some families, using a reprimand like the example above may not be an option as it is not how they would like to parent their child. As a BCBA, that is something that I have to be okay with. If Punishment is something that ever comes up, the opportunity to be able to talk about it is something that's also really important for treatment. If it does get to that point where we have run out of options and may be starting to consider using a punishment procedure in the treatment of your child, I want for you to know and be rest assured that it does not mean what you may think it does, and that punishment is simply a way of decreasing a behavior.

Punishment can really work and it can really help people if it is used correctly. Now, let's talk about the other side of punishment or of any therapy, really. Even though you do all that you need to do and it is working in the moment, the reality is that it may not work forever. In ABA, a lot of what we do is pivot whenever things aren't going the way we expect them too. There is a lot of pivoting throughout the entire process of treatment. When using punishment, it may be the same. If it's not working, change it, and if it is, don't.

An example of punishment not working for my client is when we used a procedure called response cost. Response cost is a type of punishment procedure where wanted possessions are taken away as a consequence for not following the rules, like removing a token from their reward chart if they don't complete a task. Response cost is used often, and most of the time, I see it being used for the wrong reasons. Are we using response cost because it will decrease their behavior or are we using it because we are frustrated by the behavior that our children are engaging in, so we threaten or successfully take away the things they earned because we think that it will help? When something is taken away from us, it doesn't feel good. When something is taken away from our children, it doesn't feel good to them either.

Back when I took over a case a few years ago, I noticed the client had a token board in place. A token board is a visual tool we often use to encourage positive behavior. It usually has a board or chart, some kind of tokens like stars or stickers, and a section for the goal and reward. The way it works is pretty straightforward: whenever the child shows the desired behavior, they earn a token that goes on the board. Once they collect a certain number of tokens, they get a reward, which acts as positive reinforcement. It's a great way to provide visual motivation, encourage good behavior, and add some structure and predictability to their day. The best part is that token boards can be totally customized to fit your child's needs, and they can be really effective if it's something that works for your child. That being said, it's really easy for us as humans to say things like, 'Do you want me to take away a token?'

or 'If you do ___ again, I'm going to take a token away.' But when you say that, you're actually threatening to take something away. If your goal is to just scare them into behaving, it can backfire. Keep in mind, it only takes one time of threatening to take something away and not following through for them to learn that you're not actually going to do it.

In this case, response cost had been used where the child would lose a token if they didn't stay on task during the activity. But by that point, the child didn't want to do anything at all. They were refusing to work entirely. And honestly, I get it. I wouldn't be motivated to work either if I knew a token could be taken away every time I messed up. But since kids come to us for support, I made the call to remove the token board altogether. Punishment might have worked for this child in the beginning, but now it was stopping them from wanting to engage in any task, which defeated the purpose. So I decided to pivot and focus on building their skills using other forms of reinforcement instead and it worked.

After seeing how removing the token board helped the child re-engage, it got me thinking about how important it is to evaluate what's actually working and what's not. Sometimes, a strategy that worked in the beginning can stop being effective and even backfire. That's why it's so important to be flexible and willing to change things up when needed. At home or even with your clinician, if punishment is ever something that is considered and your clinicians talk to you about, be open to the conversation, but make sure to ask the questions that you know you need to ask.

Here are some sample questions to ask:
1. How long has the behavior been happening for?
2. What has been done to be able to decrease or increase this behavior as part of their treatment?
3. Is it happening often and what do we want to see happen if we use punishment?

Last but what I consider the most important question is:

4. Have all reinforcement options been exhausted?

Once all of these questions have been asked and there is clarity in your child's punishment procedure, the choice to begin is up to you. There is nothing wrong with the use of punishment in your child's treatment, as what we mean when we say punishment is that we are going to add or remove something to cause an unwanted behavior to decrease. That said, it's important to always monitor how your child responds and be willing to adjust as needed. What works for one child might not work for another, and sometimes what worked before may need to be reconsidered down the road. Trust your instincts, ask the tough questions, and don't be afraid to pivot if something isn't working. At the end of the day, the goal is always to find the best approach to help your child grow and succeed.

ABA At Home In Action:

1. Define Target Behaviors

- **Identify Problematic Behaviors**: Clearly specify the behaviors you wish to address, such as defiance, tantrums, or breaking rules.

- **Communicate Expectations**: Ensure your child understands which behaviors are unacceptable and why.

2. Select Effective Punishments

- **Positive Punishment**: Introduce an aversive consequence to decrease unwanted behavior (e.g., assigning additional chores or reducing playtime). (See examples of Positive Punishment below)
  - o **Overcorrection:** This involves having the individual correct the consequences of their inappropriate behavior, often by repeating the correct behavior

multiple times. For example, if a child makes a mess, they might be required to clean it up and then clean an additional area.

- ○ **Response Blocking:** This involves physically preventing a maladaptive behavior from occurring. For instance, if a child is about to hit another person, the therapist might block the movement.

- ○ **Verbal Reprimand:** A brief, firm verbal statement given immediately after the undesired behavior, such as saying "No" or "Stop" to discourage the behavior.

- **Negative Punishment**: Remove a desirable item or privilege to reduce the behavior (e.g., taking away a favorite toy or restricting access to screen time). (See examples of Negative Punishment below)

- ○ **Time-Out:** The individual is removed from a reinforcing environment for a short period, reducing the likelihood of the behavior happening again. There are different types of time-outs, such as exclusionary (removing the child from the environment) and non-exclusionary (removing the reinforcing activity).

- ○ **Response Cost:** This involves taking away a preferred item or privilege after the undesired behavior occurs. For instance, if a child engages in inappropriate behavior, they might lose access to a favorite toy or activity.

- ○ **Removal of Attention:** This involves withdrawing attention when the undesired behavior occurs, also known as planned ignoring. The idea is that the behavior will decrease if it no longer results in attention.

3. Apply Punishments Promptly and Consistently

- **Immediate Application**: Implement the punishment immediately following the undesirable behavior to create a clear connection.

- **Maintain Consistency**: Apply punishments consistently to reinforce the behavior you want to discourage.

4. Provide Clear and Calm Explanations

- **Explain the Consequence**: Calmly clarify why the punishment is being applied (e.g., "You lost screen time because hitting is not acceptable.").

- **Focus on Learning**: Emphasize the lesson from the punishment and what behavior is expected instead (e.g., "We need to use our words, not hitting, to express our feelings.").

5. Evaluate and Adjust Approaches

- **Monitor Effectiveness**: Track the impact of punishments to determine their effectiveness and ensure they are applied consistently.

- **Adapt Strategies**: Be prepared to modify your punishment methods based on their effectiveness and your child's evolving needs.

CHAPTER 6

Influencing Behavior
Before It Begins:
Antecedent Interventions

M anaging a child's behavior and doing it so that it can provide long-term results will be the catalyst of the change. When you modify the environment, present things differently, or allow the child to, in a way, have a sense of control, it allows for behavior to potentially decrease over time, remain at low levels, or be gone for good.

This is where antecedent interventions come in. Antecedent interventions involve altering the environment before the behavior of concern occurs, with the goal of preventing it from happening. Even though, as BCBAs, we are trained to manage behavior and have various techniques at our disposal, a major focus of our work is on using antecedent interventions to prevent challenging behaviors before they occur. This means that we want to set you up for success so that the behavior doesn't need to happen.

We use antecedent interventions with children with autism because these strategies proactively address the root causes of challenging behaviors before they occur. For instance, if your child has a five- to ten-minute tantrum—or longer—every time a toy is removed, antecedent interventions are ideal for addressing this behavior because they help prevent the tantrum before it even starts. This approach is often more effective and less disruptive than reactive methods, which address behaviors after they have already happened.

Antecedent interventions may not be required when the child's behavior is consistently appropriate and manageable, if challenging behaviors occur infrequently without clear triggers, when the behavior is socially appropriate and serves a positive function, or when existing routines and strategies are already effective.

Key components of antecedent interventions involve figuring out what triggers problematic behaviors and making changes to the environment to reduce those triggers. This might mean altering physical settings, adjusting schedules, or removing things that could cause stress. We also use prompts and cues—whether verbal, visual, or physical—to guide individuals toward the right behavior. Teaching alternative behaviors helps them learn better ways to handle situations instead of falling into problematic patterns. Plus, adjusting schedules and routines can help minimize those triggers and encourage positive behavior, making the environment more predictable and supportive so potential issues are addressed before they even start.

For example, if the behavior is happening during a transition—the process of moving from one activity, place, or situation to another—one thing that we might do is establish some sort of routine, set some sort of schedule, or even use some sort of technique to be able to let the client know that the transition is going to happen. Again, we want to set you up for success so that the behavior doesn't need to happen. Something else that we may want to do is modify the environment. So maybe, if the behavior is happening when leaving the room, will the door already being open help you out when it is time? Probably, right? On the contrary, if you know that your child has a hard time transitioning and you have to go through the steps of opening a door when your child is already engaging in some sort of behavior, will the task of opening the door make it harder? Probably. Again, the goal of antecedent interventions is to prevent the behavior from happening.

If your child has a hard time transitioning away from some of their favorite toys, an antecedent intervention that you can use is placing some of their favorite toys in the area that you want them to transition to. For example, if all of their favorite toys are in their playroom, chances are they are going to have a really hard time transitioning away from that playroom. If the goal is to transition them to the bathroom because it's time to shower, or to the kitchen because it's time to eat, keeping some of their higher preferred toys in those two rooms may help.

Another tool that I recommend to families is the use of timers. Timers are a tool that we may not think to use with our kids, but the reason they help is because if children understand what timers are, they know that something is going to end, which then means that it can help with removing a preferred item, a transition, or anything else they may be struggling with. When using a timer, we are giving them a signal that there is change coming, which allows for them to prepare for it however they need to.

An example of when I used timers with one of my families was when I had a child who was having a really hard time being away from their mom. This mom couldn't be in her room for more than a few seconds without the child needing to be right next to her. My recommendation to the mom was to use a timer when she wanted to go to her room, starting by setting it for just a few seconds. For this specific child, what worked at first was only 10 seconds. They could only tolerate being away from their mom for 10 seconds, and since that's all they could handle, 10 seconds is what we went with. Mom immediately went to work implementing this. When mom set the timer, she also let her child know that she would be right back. With this, it is important to note that it is really, really important for you to not only have a signal that something is going to end, but also to let them know that it is going to end, so some sort of vocalization telling them. Having both the timer and letting the child know that Mom will be right back is important because, at some point, we want the child to be okay with just hearing that from her, without the timer. The goal is for the child to wait and be okay with waiting after Mom tells them she'll be right back. In other words, we want to eventually fade out the timer and not have to use it anymore. Once the timer went off, I told Mom to go out and greet her child, give them some praise for waiting, and say some words of affirmation that the child loves.

When implementing a target like this, where the set goal is very small—10 seconds in this case—it's important to note that it will not always be this small. The reason we start with such a small goal is because right now, that may be all that they are able to tolerate, meaning they do not have any sort of reaction, and that is okay. Once your child is able to tolerate the 10 seconds successfully, it is okay to add more time. With this client, I did tell mom that whenever it was consistent for three days to increase the timer to 20 seconds. You may be thinking, why only increase it by 10 seconds? And the answer that I have for you is this: If you add only 10 seconds to the timer the change is not as noticeable as if you added one *minute*. In some cases though, even 10 seconds may be too much. When increasing the amount of time that your child is waiting or tolerating, you never want to increase the amount of time by a lot too fast. If you do, it could lead to unwanted behavior and then potentially having to start over.

Generally, two to three days of your child tolerating the amount of time successfully without any challenging behavior is typically a good sign that you can increase it. When starting off, you may not be sure how long to set the timer for. In your case, maybe 10 seconds is too little. A way to figure out the length of time you want to start with is by trying it a few times with them. For example, telling them, "I'll be right back," and then timing on your end how long they can tolerate before they engage in some unwanted behavior. For this specific example, you'll know your child isn't able to tolerate you leaving when they start to engage in the behaviors you want to decrease. Doing this a few times can give you a good idea of what a good starting time may be. Once you figure out that time, lower it by a few seconds. For example, if the average amount of time they were able to tolerate is one minute, then setting your timer for 50 or 55 seconds gives your child the opportunity to earn the reward that you are going to be giving them.

Mom continued to use a timer, and we were able to increase the amount of time that was on the timer during the two weeks that I was working with them. At the end of the two weeks, Mom and I had a follow-up call and she let me know that her child was no longer experiencing any form of anxiety whenever she asked them to wait. They were waiting for her for up to 30 minutes and mom was able to complete things in her room without being interrupted. This is a huge win after having a child that, at first, could not be apart from mom for more than 10 seconds.

Over time, mom did not need to use a timer or even let the child know that she would be going away. The child grew to tolerate this.

Antecedent interventions are a huge tool that you can use with your child. It's just a matter of figuring out what works for your child so you can set them up for success so they won't have to engage in an unwanted behavior.

I have compiled a list of antecedent interventions and their advantages so you can choose one or a few that could work for you to implement with your child.

Examples of Antecedent Interventions:

- **Environmental Modifications:** Adjusting seating arrangements, reducing noise levels, or removing distracting items to create a conducive environment.

- **Visual Schedules:** Using visual timetables or charts to help individuals understand and predict daily activities, reducing anxiety and uncertainty.

- **Choice Making:** Allowing individuals to make choices about their activities or tasks to increase engagement and reduce resistance.

- **Priming:** Preparing individuals for upcoming events or transitions by discussing or practicing what will happen beforehand.

- **Non-Contingent Reinforcement (NCR):** Providing regular access to preferred activities or items independent of behavior, to reduce the motivation for problematic behavior.

- **Demand Fading:** Gradually increasing the difficulty or duration of tasks to build tolerance and reduce task avoidance behaviors.

Key Components of Antecedent Interventions:

- **Identifying Triggers:** Understanding the specific antecedents or triggers that lead to problematic behaviors.

- **Modifying the Environment:** Changing aspects of the environment to reduce the likelihood of the behavior occurring.

- **Providing Prompts and Cues:** Using verbal, visual, or physical prompts to guide appropriate behavior.

- **Teaching Alternative Behaviors:** Equipping individuals with alternative, appropriate behaviors to replace the problematic ones.

- **Adjusting Schedules and Routines:** Structuring activities and routines to minimize triggers and promote positive behavior.

Benefits of Antecedent Interventions:

- **Proactive Approach:** Addresses potential issues before they lead to problematic behavior.

- **Reduced Need for Reactive Measures:** Minimizes the reliance on corrective or punitive measures by preventing behaviors from occurring.

- **Enhanced Learning and Engagement:** Creates a more supportive and predictable environment conducive to learning and positive interaction.

- **Individualized Support:** Tailored to the specific needs and triggers of the individual, making interventions more effective.

CHAPTER 7

Navigating Transitions with Ease

I n the chapter about antecedent interventions, I talked about transitions. For kids with autism, transitions can be tough because they really thrive on routine and predictability. Whether it's moving from one activity to the next, switching classrooms, or even going through bigger life changes, these shifts can bring a lot of anxiety and uncertainty. That's why it's so important for parents and caregivers to help prepare and support them during transitions to make things less stressful and help everything go a little smoother.

Advance preparation plays a crucial role in easing transitions for children with autism. This includes providing ample time for preparation and familiarization with the upcoming change, such as visiting new environments, meeting new teachers or caregivers, and exploring the transition process through visual supports like schedules and social stories. By offering predictability and structure, parents can help alleviate anxiety and facilitate a more comfortable transition experience for their child.

I have compiled some ways that you can help your child cope with transitions, many of which are antecedent interventions previously learned about, and they include:

1. **Visual schedules:** Use visual aids such as pictures, icons, or written words to outline the sequence of activities or events throughout the day. This can help the child understand what to expect and reduce anxiety about upcoming transitions.

2. **Countdown timers:** Set timers or alarms to signal when a transition is approaching. Giving the child a visual or auditory cue can help them prepare for the change in activity.

3. **Social stories:** Create personalized stories or narratives that explain upcoming transitions or changes in routine in a simple and concrete way. Social stories can help the child understand why transitions are happening and what to expect during them.

4. **First-then boards:** Use a visual representation of "first" and "then" to help the child understand the sequence of activities. For example, "First we finish breakfast, then we go to school."

5. **Transition objects:** Provide a special object or item that the child can hold or interact with during transitions to provide comfort and familiarity.

6. **Breaks and transition warnings:** Offer warnings or breaks before transitions occur to give the child time to mentally prepare for the change. This can help reduce anxiety and resistance.

7. **Consistent routines:** Establish consistent daily routines and schedules to provide a sense of stability and predictability

for the child. Consistency can help reduce stress and anxiety associated with transitions.

8. **Positive reinforcement:** Offer praise, rewards, or incentives for successfully navigating transitions to reinforce positive behavior and encourage cooperation.

9. **Sensory supports:** Consider the child's sensory needs and preferences when planning transitions. Providing sensory supports, such as fidget toys, headphones, or calming activities, can help the child regulate their emotions during transitions.

10. **Collaboration and communication:** Work closely with educators, therapists, and other caregivers to develop and implement effective transition strategies. Regular communication and collaboration can help ensure consistency and support across different environments.

It's important to individualize and tailor these tools and strategies to fit the unique needs and preferences of your child. By paying close attention to what your child is good at and where they might struggle, you can find the best ways to support them and make transitions smoother.

Imagine a child with autism who's used to the familiar routine of their elementary school environment. They know their teachers, the layout of the classrooms, and the daily schedule like the back of their hand. Now, picture them facing the big transition to middle school. The bustling hallways, new class schedules, and larger student body can feel overwhelming. It's like their whole world is getting a major shake-up. Suddenly, they have to navigate unfamiliar surroundings, get used to new teachers, and follow a more complicated schedule. This abrupt shift can stir up a lot of anxiety, sensory overload, and difficulty adjusting to the new demands. As a result, they might have meltdowns, pull away from others, or resist going to school. This shows just how tough transitions can be for children with autism and highlights the need for tailored support to help them manage these changes with a sense of confidence and resilience.

And it's not just about school transitions. As children with autism approach adulthood, preparing for major life milestones becomes crucial. The transition to new environments, responsibilities, and social expectations can be pretty intimidating. This is where parents and caregivers come in. By creating comprehensive transition plans that include goals, supports, and resources, and by providing life skills training in areas like budgeting and time management, parents can give their child the tools they need to navigate these changes. Teaching self-advocacy skills is also key, as it helps the child express their needs and preferences clearly. With the right support and preparation, parents can help their child face these transitions with confidence, making the path to adulthood a bit smoother and more successful.

Similar to the list I talked about with overall transitions, I also created one specifically for you to serve as a resource to help your child with their transition into adulthood. These resources can offer guidance, support, and tools for navigating the challenges and opportunities that come with this life stage.

Education and Training:

1. **Vocational Rehabilitation Services**:
   ○ Many states have vocational rehabilitation (VR) services that help individuals with disabilities, including autism, prepare for, obtain, and maintain employment. These services can include job coaching, resume building, interview preparation, and more.
2. **Transition Programs**:
   ○ Programs like Think College offer resources for postsecondary education options for individuals with

intellectual and developmental disabilities, including autism.

o Autism Speaks has a Postsecondary Educational Opportunities Guide which lists various college programs designed for students with autism.

Employment Support:

1. **Job Placement Services**:
   o Organizations like Project SEARCH provide job training and employment opportunities for young adults with developmental disabilities.
   o autism Speaks Employment Tool Kit offers guidance on finding and securing a job, disclosing a diagnosis, and managing workplace relationships.
2. **Job Accommodation Network (JAN)**:
   o JAN offers free, expert, and confidential guidance on workplace accommodations and disability employment issues.

Independent Living:

1. **Housing and Urban Development (HUD) Programs**:
   o HUD provides resources for affordable housing and independent living arrangements. Look for local HUD offices that offer assistance specific to individuals with disabilities.
2. **Independent Living Centers**:
   o These centers provide services such as independent living skills training, peer counseling, and advocacy. The National Council on Independent Living (NCIL) can help locate a center nearby.

Social and Community Support:

1. **Social Skills Training**:
   o Programs like PEERS (Program for the Education and Enrichment of Relational Skills) offer evidence-based social skills training for young adults with autism.
2. **Support Groups**:
   o Many organizations, such as the autism Society and local autism organizations, offer support groups for adults with autism and their families.

Financial and Legal Resources:

1. **Supplemental Security Income (SSI) and Social Security Disability Insurance (SSDI)**:
   o These programs provide financial support for individuals with disabilities. The Social Security Administration can offer more information on eligibility and application processes.
2. **ABLE Accounts**:
   o Achieving a Better Life Experience (ABLE) accounts allow individuals with disabilities to save money for disability-related expenses without affecting their SSI or Medicaid eligibility.
3. **Guardianship and Alternatives**:
   o Understanding legal guardianship and exploring alternatives such as supported decision-making can be crucial for some individuals. Organizations like The Arc provide resources and information on these topics.

Healthcare and Mental Health Services:

1. **Centers for Autism and Related Disorders (CARD)**:
   o CARD offers comprehensive services for individuals with autism, including therapy, skills training, and family support.
2. **Mental Health Services**:
   o Ensuring access to mental health services is important for managing anxiety, depression, and other mental health issues that can arise during transitions. The National Alliance on Mental Illness (NAMI) can provide resources and support.

Online Resources and Tools:

1. **Autism Speaks Transition Tool Kit**:
   o This comprehensive tool kit offers guidance on various aspects of transitioning to adulthood, including employment, education, and independent living.
2. **OAR's (Organization for autism Research) "Life Journey Through autism" Series**:
   o This series includes guides specifically designed for individuals with autism and their families to navigate adulthood transitions.
3. **Interactive autism Network (IAN)**:
   o IAN provides research-based information and resources for adults with autism and their families.

Advocacy and Legal Rights:

1. **Disability Rights Organizations**:
   - Organizations like Disability Rights Education and Defense Fund (DREDF) provide information on legal rights and advocacy for individuals with disabilities.
2. **Americans with Disabilities Act (ADA)**:
   - Understanding the protections and accommodations provided under the ADA can help individuals with autism advocate for themselves in education, employment, and public life.

For an even more extended list of resources, please visit www.promptpathconsulting. com/resources.

Please keep in mind that service locations and availability can vary. It's a good idea to contact each organization directly to get the most accurate and up-to-date information about what they offer and where. Always double-check with the organizations or local directories to ensure you have the latest details.

Navigating tough transitions with a child with autism is all about patience, understanding, and being proactive. First things first, keep those lines of communication wide open. Acknowledge how your child feels about the upcoming change—whether it's moving to a new school, starting a new therapy, or any big shift in their routine. Let them know it's okay to share their worries and fears.

Create a supportive environment where your child feels safe to express their concerns. Visual supports can be a game-changer here. Use schedules, social stories, or transition timelines to give your child a clear picture of what to expect. This can help ease their anxiety by making the unknown a little less intimidating.

Practice is key. Offer chances for your child to rehearse or get used to the new environment before the actual change happens. This might mean role-playing scenarios or visiting the new place ahead of time. It's all about helping them feel more comfortable and prepared.

Work closely with teachers, therapists, and anyone else in your support network to come up with personalized strategies that fit your child's unique needs and preferences. Consistent reassurance and encouragement will go a long way in helping your child adjust. Tailor your support to make the transition smoother and boost their confidence as they adapt.

Remember, every child's journey is unique, so don't hesitate to seek extra guidance if you need it. By creating a nurturing and supportive atmosphere, you're setting the stage for your child to embrace change with courage and flexibility.

In the next chapter, we'll dive into communication strategies and tools that can help your child express their needs and emotions more effectively. Improving communication can make a big difference in interactions and behavior management, setting up a solid foundation for positive change.

CHAPTER 8

Empower & Enhance Communication Skills

E very child is one-of-a-kind, so the challenges you might face in supporting your child's communication will vary. Finding the right strategies that fit your child's unique needs is crucial. As we dive into this journey of boosting your child's communication and social skills, keep a few key things in mind. Patience and consistency are your best friends—progress takes time, and every little victory is worth celebrating. Customize your approach to fit what works for your child, because what's effective for one might not be for another. Work closely with professionals like speech-language pathologists and therapists to create a well-rounded plan for your child's growth. Together, we'll navigate this path and support your child's journey every step of the way.

When talking about communication, I use the terms nonverbal and nonvocal. Each of them mean different things. Non-vocal means that they are not able to vocalize or talk with words, and nonverbal means that they are not able to communicate in any way and are not able to express their wants and needs at all. I made it a point to mention this because when we talk about communication, we typically say that our child is nonverbal when we may actually mean nonvocal. This distinction is especially important when it comes to the way your child demands or makes a request.

For me, the most important thing I focus on when I start working with a new client is manding. Manding, which you will hear a lot if your child is in ABA therapy, simply means making a request. When a child mands, it means they are requesting something either from you or in general. Manding is the most important skill I will ever teach one of my clients because the way we communicate is crucial in life. It allows a child to express their wants and needs and, as a human being, to communicate effectively.

When I start a new case, something I look at is what their maladaptive behaviors are like and how much they're able to communicate. I examine this because, in most cases, a child's behavior is directly correlated with how much or how little they are able to communicate. Typically, when a clinician starts teaching your child to mand or communicate, you will most often see their maladaptive behavior decrease. This will not happen in every case, but from my experience and with most of my cases, this is what I have observed.

For example, if your child's screaming or tantrums were originally a way to get your attention, and they've now learned to ask for attention by saying 'hey' or by tapping your arm, they no longer need to resort to screaming or tantrums. With this new way to communicate, the need for the old behavior fades away. Essentially, as your child learns more effective communication skills, the old behaviors that served the same purpose will decrease. Working on improving their communication can help reduce those challenging behaviors.

Now, let's dive into some effective approaches for your child to be able to communicate together.

Following, we will talk about:

1. Speech and vocal communication
2. Gestures, body language, and facial expressions
3. Augmented and Alternative Communication (AAC) Devices
4. American Sign Language
5. Picture or icon exchange
6. Written communication

Speech and Vocal Communication:

Speech and vocal communication means that your child is using words to express their needs and feelings. When your child begins to talk, you might notice different patterns of communication. For instance, echolalia is one such pattern where your child repeats words or phrases they've heard. This repetition can be a way for them to process language and communicate. However, echolalia is just one aspect of speech development and doesn't mean it will be the only way your child communicates forever.

Besides echolalia, there are other forms of speech and vocal communication that you might observe. Your child may start using single words or short phrases to express their needs, such as saying "milk" when they're thirsty or "car" when they want to go for a ride. These early attempts at communication are crucial milestones and show that your child is beginning to use language purposefully.

As your child's vocabulary expands, you'll see them stringing together more words into simple sentences, like "I want cookie" or "Mommy help me." This progression from single words to sentences is a natural part of language development. It's important to support this growth by engaging in conversations with your child, even if they're still using short phrases or single words.

Even though echolalia and other early speech patterns aren't necessarily something that needs to be "fixed," they can be guided toward more functional communication. For instance, if your child repeats, "Do you want a drink?" when they're thirsty, you can model a more functional response by saying, "I want a drink, please." This helps them learn to use language in a way that more directly communicates their needs.

Gestures, Body Language, and Facial Expressions:

In addition to verbal communication, your child might also use non-verbal methods to express themselves. These are a way that your child can communicate even if they have limited verbal abilities. Gestures such as pointing, waving, or giving a thumbs-up can convey needs, desires, and emotions without words. For instance, a child might point to a desired object to indicate they want it, or wave to greet someone. Body language, including posture and movements, can also communicate feelings and intentions, such as turning away to indicate discomfort or leaning forward to show interest. Facial expressions play a crucial role in expressing emotions like happiness, sadness, or frustration. Smiling, frowning, or raising eyebrows can provide important social and emotional cues. They may also use a specific look to show they're upset.

Teaching and encouraging the use of these nonverbal communication methods can greatly enhance your child's ability to interact and connect with others, making it easier for them to express themselves and understand social contexts. Understanding and responding to these non-verbal cues is just as important as supporting their verbal communication.

An Alternative and Augmentative Communication (AAC) Device:

AAC devices are amazing tools that give kids a way to express their thoughts, needs, and emotions in a structured format. They can range from simple communication boards with pictures and symbols to advanced electronic devices that actually generate speech. Think of AAC devices like apps on your phone or specialized gadgets designed just for communication purposes.

For instance, a child might use a tablet with an AAC app to pick out images or type messages, which the device then speaks out loud. This setup helps them join conversations, make requests, and share how they're feeling. What's great is that these devices can be customized to fit the child's likes and daily routines. This means they can really reflect what the child needs to communicate effectively with family, friends, and teachers.

It's important to use the AAC device regularly and practice with it often. The more they use it, the better they get at communicating. Over time, this can make a big difference, enhancing their communication skills and overall quality of life. By integrating these devices into their daily life, children can gain more confidence in expressing themselves and connecting with the world around them.

> For a full list of my recommended AAC
> devices and a guide on how to use them,
> go to www.promptpathconsulting.
> com/resources

Sign Language (ASL):

Sign language is a very effective way of communicating. What I tell parents when they are wanting to teach their child sign language is to keep in mind that not every person in this world communicates or understands sign language. In your immediate family, it might be something that is really great to use, as it can provide a clear and accessible way for your child to express themselves and connect with those around them.

However, it's important to remember that outside your immediate circle, such as in social settings, schools, or public places, not everyone will be familiar with sign language. This could present challenges if your child needs to communicate with people who don't know sign language. For instance, if your child uses sign language primarily at home but encounters someone who doesn't understand it, there may be communication barriers that can cause frustration for both your child and the other person involved.

I won't ever speak against sign language because it is a form of communication and it is effective. It provides a way for children to communicate their needs and interact with others, which is incredibly valuable. But I always like to let parents know about the broader context and potential limitations. By being aware of these factors, you can make an informed decision about whether sign language is the right choice for your child, considering both the immediate benefits and the practical implications for their overall communication experience.

Picture or Icon Exchange:

A child with autism can effectively communicate using the Picture Exchange Communication System (PECS), which involves exchanging pictures or icons to convey messages, needs, and desires. This method is especially useful for nonverbal children, allowing them to initiate communication by selecting and handing over a picture representing a specific item, action, or emotion. For example, if a child wants a snack, they might give a picture of a snack to a caregiver, clearly indicating their request.

PECS is particularly empowering because it gives children a way to express themselves without relying on verbal skills. This fosters greater independence and helps reduce frustration that can come from not being able to communicate their needs effectively. Over time, as your child becomes more comfortable with PECS, they can expand their vocabulary of pictures and symbols. They might start building more complex sentences, which can enhance their ability to engage in meaningful interactions with others. This visual and tangible form of communication is not only accessible but also highly adaptable, making it an invaluable tool for many children with autism.

Creating visual supports for PECS is something you can easily do at home. Typically, all you need is a laminating machine, paper, laminating sheets, and Velcro. It's a straightforward process, and you can tailor the pictures and icons to fit your child's current preferences and needs. This way, the communication system remains relevant and engaging for your child, making it even more effective in supporting their communication skills.

Written Communication:

Finally, using written communication can be a powerful tool for helping your child express their thoughts, needs, and emotions, especially if they have stronger literacy skills than vocal abilities. Writing offers a structured and often less stressful way for children to communicate. Whether they're handwriting notes, typing on a computer, or using a tablet, written communication can provide a clear outlet for expression.

For example, if your child has a hard time vocalizing their feelings or making requests, they might find it easier to write a note to their teacher or parent. This can be a way for them to say what they want, share how they're feeling, or ask questions in a way that's comfortable for them. Written communication can make it easier for children to convey complex ideas, which is particularly useful in educational settings where written assignments and responses are a regular part of the curriculum.

Encouraging your child to use writing as a form of communication not only helps in daily interactions but also supports their academic development. It can boost their confidence and independence by giving them another effective way to express themselves. By integrating written communication into their daily routine, you're helping them build essential skills that enhance their ability to communicate and navigate various aspects of life with greater ease.

Putting Communication Strategies to Action

For all of the forms of communication that I talked about above and all of those that are out there, remember, consistency is key in implementing these methods, and starting with simple, familiar concepts can help your child gradually build confidence.

Now that we have talked about different forms of communication, I now want to talk about how you can use these methods to teach your child how to mand, or request. My examples will be with vocalizations, but the example and the way to do it is the same for icons, an AAC device, ASL, and written communication.

When teaching your child how to mand, you want to start with one-word mands. Start with some of your child's favorite toys or foods. The way that you want to teach them is the same. You want to have the item available to be delivered immediately as soon as they ask for what you're offering. When you are teaching your child how to mand, especially in the very early stages of the teaching, it is okay to help them out or like I have mentioned before, speak for them. As soon as you help them and they respond in the way that you want them to, or you speak for them and they say the word that you want them to, the next thing you need to do is give them whatever item they asked for. It is important that I note that at first, you will be reinforcing responses that are not independent.

For example, let's say your child's favorite food is Goldfish. You will set up the opportunity for your child to mand by sitting or being in an area where you are able to control the item and your child. Ideally this would be having your child in a high chair or at a table where they may not easily be able to go somewhere. I call this sort of environment a controlled environment because it's controlled by you.

The next thing you will do is prompt, or help, your child to be able to say whatever word you want them to say. If you're using a device, you would have their hand touch whatever icon it is that you want them to ask for. In this example, Goldfish. Once they say or touch the icon for Goldfish, the next step is to give them Goldfish.

Once your child is able to say or touch the icon for Goldfish without your help, you can then start giving them more Goldfish based on an independent response. So if they independently ask for Goldfish, you want to give them more than one, versus if you still have to help them, you may want to only give them one. This process is called differential reinforcement and it just means that you are rewarding, even more, the independent responses. This way of teaching motivates your child to respond independently because they know that if they do, they will get more than just one of the item you're using. For example, if you are using cake, you would then give them a bigger piece of cake if they responded independently.

Once your child is fluently and independently able to communicate using one word and they are generalizing this—generalizing meaning that they are able to not only ask for the item that you first introduced, but they are also able to mand using one word for other items such as drinks, toys, actions, and other foods other than the one you first started with—you then want to have them mand using two words, and then move to three words once they master two. The process for teaching two and three words is the same as teaching one, the only difference is now you would not honor one word requests and only deliver the reinforcement for them manding using two words, three words, or even full sentences when you get there.

When your child begins treatment, you might not always see the progress in communication that you hope for right away. If that's the case, or if you're looking to give them an extra boost, consider incorporating speech therapy sessions led by qualified professionals. These sessions can offer tailored support for specific areas like speech articulation, language comprehension, and verbal expression.

In addition to formal therapy, integrating social communication interventions and language strategies into your child's daily routines is crucial. Creating a language-rich environment at home is equally important. Engage in activities like reading aloud, having conversations, and encouraging social interactions. These everyday moments provide valuable opportunities for your child to practice and reinforce their verbal skills in a familiar setting, boosting their confidence and fluency in communication.

A little secret I like to share with parents and therapists is the power of narrating throughout your day. It might seem simple, but talking through your actions and thoughts can be incredibly beneficial. Remember, just because your child isn't speaking doesn't mean they aren't listening or understanding what you're saying. By nurturing their communication skills in these ways, you're giving them the best chance to thrive.

Enhancing Communication Through Social Interaction

Social interaction is key to boosting your child's communication skills. When children have regular opportunities to socialize with others, they naturally practice and enhance their ability to express themselves. This practice helps them learn to use words and phrases more effectively and understand how to convey their thoughts and needs more clearly. For example, when your child interacts with family members or peers, they get to practice initiating conversations, responding to questions, and sharing their ideas in real-time.

Enrolling your child in social groups or structured play activities provides a supportive environment where they can engage in meaningful interactions and get used to different ways of communicating. At home, encourage your child to join in family conversations, play with friends, or participate in group activities. These everyday interactions offer practical, real-world opportunities for your child to use and refine their communication skills, building confidence and fluency in a natural and supportive setting.

Keep in mind that progress might not always be smooth. There will be bumps along the way, and setbacks are just part of the journey. But with your steadfast support and dedication, your child can push through these challenges and keep moving forward. Celebrate every little victory, no matter how small it seems, and don't forget to take care of yourself, too. You play a crucial role in your child's progress, and your love and commitment are key. By using the strategies from this book and tailoring them to fit your child's unique needs, you can help them reach their full potential and lead fulfilling lives.

ABA At Home In Action:

1. Speech and Vocal Communication

- **Encourage Conversation:** Engage in regular talks with your child and ask open-ended questions.

- **Model Clear Speech:** Use simple and clear language for your child to mimic.

2. Gestures, Body Language, and Facial Expressions

- **Use Gestures:** Incorporate gestures and body language to support understanding.

- **Be Expressive:** Show emotions through facial expressions and body language.

3. Augmented and Alternative Communication (AAC) Devices

- **Choose the Right Device:** Select an AAC device or app that fits your child's needs.

- **Teach Usage:** Guide your child in using the device regularly.

4. American Sign Language (ASL)

- **Learn Basics:** Learn and use basic ASL signs in daily interactions.

- **Practice Consistently:** Integrate ASL into everyday routines.

5. Picture or Icon Exchange and Written Communication

- **Use Picture Exchange:** Implement a picture or icon system for requests and choices.

- **Introduce Writing:** Start using simple written words for labels and instructions.

CHAPTER 9

Embarking on the Potty Training Journey

When I start my interviews with parents, I always ask them what they want to focus on. Even though I have my own ideas about what the kids should be working on, parents often notice things at home that we might not see. One answer I frequently hear is that parents want to work on toileting and getting their children potty trained.

I find that parents often bring up toileting because they've either tried it before and been unsuccessful or they're just fed up with the cost of diapers. Diapers can get really pricey, and buying them regularly can put a strain on any budget. I do approach toileting with a bit of caution, though. Sometimes, the timing just isn't right for the child, and it's important to recognize that parents might not be fully ready either.

Before we move on, I want to make it clear: it's not your fault if your child isn't potty trained by a certain age. You're doing the best you can with what you know, and it's important to recognize that.

Transitions, sitting for extended periods, dressing, and communication are some reasons why children might not be ready for potty training. From my experience with autism, transitions can be particularly challenging for kids, and the bathroom might be a tough place for them to adjust to. Sitting for a long time may not be a skill they've mastered yet. Dressing is another hurdle— they might struggle to pull down their pants and underwear, and if they have an accident, they'll need help with their clothes. Communication is also key; if they can't tell us when they need to go, it complicates the process. So, when a caregiver tells me they want to focus on toileting, I always consider these factors.

The reality is that some children may not be ready to be potty trained, and that's okay. If they're not, remember that this may not be forever, and you can always try again after working on the necessary skills.

Now, let's look at some key signs to see if your child might be ready for potty training. First, does your child seem uncomfortable in a soiled diaper? For example, they might try to take it off themselves, or you might find soiled diapers around your home. Another sign is whether your child can sit down for longer periods without difficulty. Do they walk into the bathroom without needing a reward like a favorite toy? How about diaper changes— are they smooth, or does your child resist? Finally, think about their communication skills. Even if they're not talking, can they express their needs to you? If you're answering 'yes' to many of these questions, it's a good chance your child might be ready to start potty training and it could be a great moment to take that next step.

If you answered no to most of those questions chances are your child may not be ready to be potty trained.

Beginning to potty train your child when they are not ready is not going to hurt them, but it could cause some behaviors to increase or happen altogether when maybe they weren't happening in the past. Some things that have happened when I have begun potty training when I knew the child wasn't ready, but because it was a really important request from families, are that, in one case, the child began to engage in behaviors they weren't engaging in before, which were a cause of concern. In other cases—and this is one that I experienced more frequently—the potty training process started, and we were taking them as many times as needed throughout the day, but there was no progress being made. Other times, we've seen that skills the child was making progress on can start to regress.

It's important to note that potty training is a very time-intensive task in therapy. Since the child needs to use the bathroom every 15 to 30 minutes, especially at first, this can take away from other learning opportunities.

If you are ready to take that next step after noticing all of the signs that your child may be ready, start by introducing the potty in a stress-free way. Let your child get used to it at their own pace—maybe they sit on it with their clothes on at first or you just chat about what it's for. The goal is to make the potty a familiar, non-threatening part of their space.

Once they're comfortable, set up a consistent routine. This means having regular bathroom breaks and gently encouraging them to let you know when they need to go. Routine helps build a predictable pattern and reinforces using the potty.

Patience is crucial here. Celebrate every little win, no matter how small. Whether it's sitting on the potty or actually using it, every bit of progress is a victory. Positive reinforcement, like praise or a little reward, can make the process more enjoyable and motivating.

Ultimately the goal is that we want children to be as independent as possible and we want for them to use the bathroom on their own but sometimes the reality is they just may not be ready, and like I mentioned before it is okay if they are not.

Remember, potty training is a journey, not a sprint.

ABA At Home In Action:

Identify Readiness Indicators
- Observe and assess your child's readiness for potty training by looking for key indicators.

- **Example**: Check if your child dislikes being in a soiled diaper, can sit for extended periods, transitions to the bathroom without issues, cooperates during diaper changes, and communicates needs.

Evaluate and Build Necessary Skills
- Focus on developing the essential skills required for successful potty training if your child is not yet ready.

- **Example**: Work on improving your child's ability to transition to different locations, sit still for a period, dress and undress, and communicate their needs effectively.

Create a Supportive Environment
- Set up a conducive and encouraging environment for potty training when your child shows readiness.

- **Example**: Have a comfortable and inviting bathroom setup, including a potty chair, step stool, and visual aids that can help guide your child through the process.

Gradual Introduction and Positive Reinforcement
- Introduce potty training gradually and use positive reinforcement to encourage your child.

- **Example**: Start by having your child sit on the potty at regular intervals and provide praise or small rewards for any attempts or successes.

Monitor Progress and Adjust as Needed

- Continuously monitor your child's progress and be flexible in your approach, adjusting strategies based on their needs and responses.

- **Example**: If your child shows signs of frustration or regression in other skills, consider pausing potty training and focusing on readiness skills before trying again.

For the complete potty training guide, head over to www.promptpathconsulting. com/resources and grab The Ultimate Potty Training Protocol!

CHAPTER 10

Tailoring Education to Your Child's Needs

W hen you have a child with any sort of special needs, the school they attend is really important. The reality is that not every school is going to be the best fit for your child. In some cases, a school might seem perfect but may not offer the specific type of teaching or support you need to help your child maintain the progress you've made at home. In this chapter, I'll share some insights I've gained as a clinician to help you evaluate whether the school your child is in or the one you're considering is the best fit for their needs."

The location where you live can have a big impact on the types of schools available and the programs they offer. A school in a smaller town may not have the type of classroom that you might be looking for or that your child might need. This is really important for me to note because it is one thing that I have discovered especially in the last few years. I also would like to note that homeschooling will not be covered when talking about this, and this is more specific to children that attend some sort of in-person school setting. That does not mean that homeschooling is a bad option, from personal experience, I just know that homeschooling is not possible for every child.

There are several types of settings that schools may offer for children with special needs. First, there's the inclusion classroom, where students with disabilities are integrated into general education classes alongside their typically developing peers. These classrooms focus on accommodations and support to help all students participate and succeed.

Next, there are resource rooms. These are separate classrooms where students with disabilities receive additional support, often from special education teachers or aides. Students might spend part of their day in a resource room to get individualized instruction, help with specific skills, or assistance with accommodations and modifications.

Finally, self-contained classrooms are designed for students with disabilities to receive all their instruction in a separate setting tailored to their needs. These classrooms usually have a lower student-teacher ratio and provide more intensive support.

In addition to these options, some schools are specialized and cater specifically to children with special needs or those with an Individualized Education Plan (IEP).

From my own experience, the process of securing an IEP can take some time. The first step to having an IEP for your child is for you, the parent, to request it. Sometimes, most schools won't say that your child needs it until later on in their school life, so maybe after second or third grade. As their parent, you know your child better than anyone else and if you believe in your heart that your child needs an IEP, then request it.

Something to note as well is that requesting an IEP in every single school looks different. In some cases you are able to tell their teacher that you want to request an IEP, but in other cases, the request has to be made in writing to the school district, and I am sure there are other ways some districts require you to request one that are different from the ones I mentioned. When looking to request an IEP, a good person to start with is your child's current teacher or counselor. If, at your school, they are not the person you need to go to, someone in the school's office will be able to help you out or point you in the direction of who you need to contact to request it.

After you request it, the next step is the evaluation process. The evaluation process involves gathering information about your child's academic, developmental, and functional abilities. This may include assessments conducted by psychologists, special education teachers, speech therapists, and other professionals. The purpose of the evaluation is to determine whether your child qualifies for special education services under the Individuals with Disabilities Education Act (IDEA). Some schools have a set number of days where they have to get the IEP done from the day that you requested it, however some schools do not have any sort of requirement like this, so if it has been a while since you last heard something about the IEP process, my recommendation to you is to ask about it. The next step, once the school has finished with what they need to do in order to determine IEP eligibility, is the IEP meeting itself, if your child is found eligible.

For the IEP meeting, you will be invited to attend the meeting along with relevant school personnel, such as teachers, special education providers, and administrators. The purpose of the meeting is to develop an individualized education plan for your child that outlines their educational goals, the services and accommodations they will receive, and how progress will be measured. One thing that parents aren't always aware of is that your child is able to attend that meeting too. If your child is older or able to express their thoughts on the goals that are being put in place for them, them attending can also help set them up for success. In order for I, your BCBA to be a part of that meeting, most times, all that you as the parent have to do is request that I be there. During the IEP meeting, the team will discuss your child's strengths, needs, and goals for academic and functional development. They will also determine the appropriate special education services, accommodations, and modifications to support your child's learning. The resulting document will be the IEP, which is a legally binding document outlining the specific services and supports your child will receive.

The classroom setting that your child will be in will also be determined during that meeting. This decision will be based on the different assessments that were done. If you believe that your child needs to be in a special education classroom, but the IEP doesn't say so, then your child will not be in a special education classroom. If that is something that you feel like your child needs, then please make sure to say something during the IEP meeting.

If it's not written on their IEP, it will not happen.

IEP meetings can be lengthy and overwhelming, however, rest assured that everyone in that meeting wants what's best for your child. As their parent or caregiver, if you don't agree with some of the goals that are in your child's IEP, or if you want more goals added than what is in place, you have a right to say so. I always tell my families, "Don't be afraid to advocate even more for your child."

Once the IEP is developed, the school will begin implementing the services and accommodations outlined in the plan. Progress will be monitored regularly, and the IEP team will meet annually to review your child's progress, make any necessary adjustments to the plan, and set new goals as needed. One thing about their IEP that I believe is important to note is that you have a right to request another IEP meeting during that same school year if you are noticing changes in your child that weren't happening before.

You know your child better than anyone else. I want to make sure that you know that. Sometimes having a child with special needs can make the education system a little bit more complicated, but your child is in the right setting if they are trying their best to meet their needs. Don't be afraid to advocate for your child to have an IEP and for them to be in the setting that you believe will work best for them. Schools are meant to set your children up for success and I know from experience that most teachers and administrators will do their very best to do that. There are times where they won't be able to, but the decision to move your child to a different school will be yours entirely.

If an IEP isn't the right fit for your child or if they need a different kind of support, you might consider a 504 Plan. A 504 Plan provides accommodations and modifications to help your child succeed in the general education environment without the more extensive services that an IEP might include. It's designed to ensure that students with disabilities have equal access to educational opportunities. This plan can make a significant difference in helping your child navigate their school experience with the support they need.

ABA At Home In Action:

Assess School Fit and Offerings

- Evaluate whether the schools in your area provide the necessary classroom settings and resources for your child's needs.

Request an Individualized Education Plan (IEP)

- Initiate the process of obtaining an IEP for your child if you believe they need special education services.

Participate in the IEP Process

- Actively engage in the IEP evaluation and meeting process to ensure your child's needs are accurately assessed and addressed.

Advocate for Appropriate Services and Supports

- Advocate for the services, accommodations, and classroom settings that best support your child's learning and development.

Monitor and Review Progress

- Regularly monitor your child's progress and request additional IEP meetings if needed to address any changes or new needs.

CHAPTER 11

Creating Peaceful Bedtime Routines

Bedtime can be a tough time for any parent, but it can be especially challenging for those with children with autism. Kids with autism might have trouble winding down, be extra sensitive to sensory stimuli, or deal with anxiety that makes falling asleep feel overwhelming.

The most common question I get from the families I work with is, "Should I give them melatonin?" What I will say is that I am not a doctor, and as a parent, you should do what you believe is best for your child, but I will always encourage you to consult their doctor. They know your child's medical history best and can give you some guidance with this question.

I remember working with a family whose child struggled with bedtime routines. The child, let's call him Jake, had a hard time winding down, which often led to lengthy bedtime battles. We started by observing Jake's current routine and noticed a few key things: his room was a bit overstimulating with bright lights and loud toys, and he had a hard time transitioning from one activity to another.

We simplified Jake's bedtime routine to suit his needs better. We started by creating a calming environment with dimmed lights and soothing sounds, like gentle music or white noise. We set up a consistent sequence—warm bath, reading a book, and quiet time with a soft toy.

To help Jake understand what to expect, we used a visual bedtime chart with pictures. We practiced the routine during the day to ease his anxiety and praised him each night for following it.

It wasn't an overnight fix, but with patience and consistency, Jake adapted well. The predictable, calming environment made bedtime smoother and more positive for him.

In this chapter, I'll share some tips and strategies I've picked up from my work as a clinician to help you set up a successful bedtime routine for your child with autism.

First and foremost, having a consistent and predictable bedtime routine can make a big difference. Kids with autism often find comfort in predictability, which helps reduce anxiety and makes them feel secure. A structured routine lets your child know it's time to transition from the day's activities to a restful night's sleep.

We all want our kids to have a good night's sleep, but sometimes winding down can be a real struggle. Whether it's trouble settling down, heightened sensitivity to sensory inputs, or anxiety about falling asleep, the bedtime routine becomes crucial.

So, where do you start? First things first, set a regular bedtime and wake-up time, even on weekends. It might seem small, but consistency helps your child's internal clock get on track, making it easier for them to fall asleep and wake up naturally. Start the bedtime routine about 30 to 60 minutes before the desired sleep time.

Begin with a calming activity that your child enjoys. This might be reading a favorite book, listening to soothing music, or engaging in quiet playtime. Skip the screen time and vigorous play, as they can make it harder for your child to wind down. A warm bath can be a great part of this routine, as it helps relax muscles and signals that it's almost time for bed. If your child isn't a fan of baths, you could try a warm washcloth wipe-down instead.

Brushing teeth should be a predictable and positive part of the routine. Using a timer or a favorite song can help ensure that they brush for the full two minutes. If your child is sensitive to toothpaste flavors or toothbrush textures, try out different options to find what works best.

Let your child pick their pajamas if they can. Comfortable, soft pajamas can make a big difference, and giving them a choice helps them feel in control and more at ease.

End the routine with something soothing, like reading a bedtime story or singing a lullaby. Choose calming stories or songs and avoid anything too exciting or stimulating.

Creating a sleep-friendly environment is also key. Make sure their bed is comfortable and consider weighted blankets if that helps your child feel secure. If they're sensitive to light or noise, use blackout curtains and a white noise machine to create a peaceful sleep environment. Keep the room at a comfortable temperature— neither too hot nor too cold.

If your child struggles with bedtime or wakes up during the night, stay calm and reassuring. I know, this is way easier said than done, but now that you're aware, give it a try. Gentle comfort or a soft, soothing phrase can help them settle back to sleep. Consistency is crucial here—having a simple, steady response to night wakings helps your child know what to expect and settle down more easily.

Teach your child some basic relaxation techniques, like deep breathing or guided imagery. These can help calm their mind and body before bed. If your child has specific sensory sensitivities, incorporating sensory tools like a weighted blanket or a soft toy might provide extra comfort.

Establishing a consistent pre-bedtime routine can reduce anxiety and help your child feel safe and ready for sleep. It might take some time to find what works best, but it's worth it for a good night's rest. A well-structured bedtime routine supports your child's overall well-being and development, and with your patience and dedication, you can help make bedtime smoother for everyone.

Remember, you know your child best. With a bit of perseverance and a lot of love, you can create a bedtime routine that works for your family.

I've put together a list to help you with your child's bedtime routine, so feel free to use it as a resource.

ABA At Home In Action:

Creating a Consistent Bedtime Routine:

1. **Wind-Down Time**
2. **Bath Time**
3. **Oral Hygiene**
4. **Changing into Pajamas**
5. **Bedtime Story or Song**

Creating a Sleep-Friendly Environment:

1. **Comfortable Bedding**
2. **Lighting**
3. **Noise Control**
4. **Temperature**

Dealing with Sleep Resistance and Night Waking

1. Gradual Transition
2. Positive Reinforcement
3. Calming Techniques
4. Consistent Response

Addressing Anxiety and Sensory Sensitivities

1. Relaxation Techniques
2. Sensory Tools
3. Consistent Pre-Bedtime Routine
4. Professional Support

CHAPTER 12

Optimizing Mealtimes and Feeding Experiences

Navigating mealtime with a child with autism can be quite a challenge. Sensory sensitivities, strong preferences, and resistance to changes in routine often complicate feeding. From my experience as a clinician, I've gathered some practical strategies to help make mealtime a more positive experience for your family. In this chapter, we'll explore these challenges and dive into actionable tips to support your child's nutritional needs and overall well-being.

First off, it's crucial to know that children with autism often have heightened sensory sensitivities that can impact their eating habits. The texture, taste, smell, and even appearance of food can sometimes be overwhelming. Start by observing what specific aspects of food might be causing issues for your child. Once you have a clearer picture, you can begin to make changes gradually and in a way that feels manageable.

One approach that often works well is introducing new foods slowly and in small amounts. Pairing a new food with something your child already likes can make the new food seem less intimidating. For example, if your child loves apples but is unsure about carrots, try serving a small piece of carrot alongside their favorite apple slices. Encourage them to touch, smell, and eventually taste the new food, but avoid pressuring them. Repeated exposure, without force, can help them feel more comfortable with new foods over time.

One of my favorite experiences during a feeding intervention involved a three-year-old child. This child's diet consisted of Cheetos, pancakes, applesauce or baby food, and milk. The choices of food that this child selected were also very inconsistent, as some days they wanted them and other days they did not. The one consistent food that was offered to them that they would eat every single time was Cheetos. Their caregiver came to me concerned about the selection of foods that she was allowing her child to eat. Because the child's favorite food was Cheetos, I decided to start the feeding process with other types of chips that had the same consistency as a Cheeto, including Cheeto puffs because it was of the same family.

As expected, when attempting to feed them the other chips, the child did not respond positively. The only chip they wanted out of the selection of six different chips was their Cheetos. The presentation of different chips did not result in a positive reaction, so we took a step back and moved to trying to have them touch any of the other chips. After a few trials of trying to have them touch the chip, they did it. Touching the chip meant that the reward they were going to receive was one of their Cheetos.

We continued this process over two weeks. After successfully touching the chips every time we asked them to for one week, the next step was to move to putting the chip to their mouth. We began by showing them to put it to their mouth and then we moved to showing they could eat it. We did this for a three days and on the fourth day, they put a chip in their mouth. They did not chew or swallow it, in fact they immediately took it out, but that was a huge win for us. When they did this, we threw a party. Not only did we give them two Cheetos, but we also celebrated that they did something they had never done before. We gave high fives, hugs, praise, and carried them. We did these things to serve as positive reinforcement because we want to see that behavior (putting other chips in their mouth) increase.

It took five weeks for them to consistently eat other types of chips. After five weeks, the child was also no longer engaging in maladaptive behaviors when we presented other chips that were not their Cheetos. Working on feeding with your child will take you some time, but if you remain consistent and work on it every single day your child could make progress.

> To download the exact protocol
> I used with this client go to
> www.promptpathconsulting.
> com/resources.

Making mealtime work for your child with autism can be a real challenge, but with a bit of creativity and patience, it can get better. Setting up a consistent and predictable mealtime routine is a big help. When your child knows what to expect, it can ease their anxiety and make mealtime smoother. Try using visual schedules or social stories to lay out the mealtime steps—like washing hands, setting the table, eating, and cleaning up. This can give your child a sense of order and control.

Creating a calm dining environment also makes a difference. Keep the area quiet and free from distractions to help your child focus on their food. Some kids might benefit from sensory tools, like a weighted lap pad or a special cushion, to help them feel settled at the table.

Get your child involved in preparing meals if you can. Simple tasks like washing veggies, stirring ingredients, or setting the table can make them feel more invested in mealtime. Plus, it's a great way to introduce new foods in a non-threatening way.

Positive reinforcement can work wonders too. Praise and rewards for small steps—like touching, smelling, or tasting new foods—can motivate your child. Whether it's immediate praise, a small treat, or part of a reward system, showing appreciation can encourage them to try new things.

If your child is very picky, it's all about patience and experimenting. Start by offering different types of foods within the same category of what they already like. For example, if they love crackers, try different kinds or textures of crackers. Gradually introduce new textures and flavors.

Make sure your child's diet is balanced, too. If their limited eating is causing nutritional issues, check with a pediatrician or nutritionist. They can suggest supplements or diet tweaks to make sure your child's getting what they need.

Sometimes feeding problems can be linked to medical issues your child might not be able to communicate. If you suspect this might be the case, consult specialists for advice.

Mealtime with a child with autism can be tricky, but with some trial and error, you can make it a more enjoyable part of your routine. Stay patient, keep things consistent, and adjust your approach based on what works best for your child. Progress might be slow, but with perseverance and understanding, you can help your child develop better eating habits and enjoy mealtimes more.

ABA At Home In Action:

1. Establish a Consistent Routine

- **Set Regular Meal Times:** Create a predictable schedule for meals and snacks to build consistency and reduce anxiety.

- **Prepare in Advance:** Plan and prep meals ahead of time to minimize stress during feeding.

2. Create a Comfortable Eating Environment

- **Minimize Distractions:** Ensure the eating area is calm and free from distractions like loud noises or clutter.

- **Use Preferred Utensils:** Choose utensils and dishes that your child finds comfortable and easy to use.

3. Incorporate Visual and Social Supports

- **Use Visual Schedules:** Implement visual schedules or picture menus to help your child understand what to expect.

- **Model Eating Behavior:** Demonstrate eating behaviors and encourage imitation by eating the same foods together.

4. Introduce New Foods Gradually

- **Start Slowly:** Introduce new foods in small amounts alongside familiar favorites to reduce resistance.

- **Offer Choices:** Allow your child to choose from a limited selection of foods to encourage participation and reduce anxiety.

5. Provide Positive Reinforcement

- **Praise and Reward:** Offer positive reinforcement and praise for trying new foods or eating independently.

- **Use a Reward System:** Implement a reward system to motivate and reinforce positive eating behaviors and to celebrate their wins.

CHAPTER 13

Embracing and Celebrating Your Child's Uniqueness

mbracing and celebrating the uniqueness of children with autism is not just about acknowledging their differences but actively supporting their growth and fostering a sense of inclusivity. When we make a concerted effort to recognize and value the individual traits of these children, we're doing more than just appreciating them for who they are—we're laying the groundwork for their overall development and for a more accepting society.

The Importance of Embracing Individuality

Understanding and embracing the individuality of children with autism is a powerful way to bolster their self-esteem and well-being. Every child is a unique individual with their own set of strengths, preferences, and challenges. By celebrating these traits, we're helping them build a positive self-image that's crucial for their confidence and sense of identity. When we highlight and celebrate their unique qualities, we're sending a clear message: their differences are not only accepted but valued.

This approach has far-reaching benefits. It empowers children with autism to take pride in who they are and encourages them to explore their interests and passions. By doing so, they're more likely to engage in activities that foster their growth and development. Plus, this positive reinforcement can motivate them to pursue their goals, whether it's developing a special talent, diving into a hobby, or simply feeling more comfortable and accepted in their social circles.

Fostering Inclusivity and Acceptance

Celebrating individuality doesn't just impact the child with autism—it also has broader societal implications. When we actively embrace and respect diversity, we contribute to creating a more inclusive society. This kind of acceptance helps to normalize differences and encourages empathy and understanding among peers, family members, and the community at large. It's about setting the stage for a world where diversity is not only acknowledged but celebrated, and where every child has the opportunity to thrive.

Nurturing Your Child's Strengths

To truly support your child's development, it's important to take a thoughtful and supportive approach to identifying and nurturing their strengths. Start by paying close attention to what excites and engages your child. Observe their reactions and preferences during various activities to understand their interests and talents. Create an environment where they feel safe and encouraged to explore different activities. Whether it's through art, music, or sports, providing a variety of experiences allows your child to discover what they enjoy and excel in.

Positive reinforcement plays a key role in this process. Offer specific, constructive feedback and celebrate even the smallest achievements. This helps to build their confidence and motivates them to keep trying. Praise their efforts and accomplishments, and be sure to recognize their unique contributions. Acknowledging their progress not only boosts their self-esteem but also reinforces their motivation to pursue their interests.

Building a Positive Self-Image

A positive self-image is essential for children with autism to navigate the world with confidence and resilience. Focus on their strengths and the things they do well. Highlight their positive qualities and how they contribute to their family and community. Encourage them to express themselves through various creative outlets like drawing, writing, or music. These activities provide a means for them to communicate their feelings and ideas in a way that's true to who they are.

Teaching your child to advocate for themselves is another important step. Help them understand how to express their needs and preferences clearly and confidently. This not only ensures their needs are met but also empowers them to take charge of their own well-being.

Creating a Supportive Environment

Fostering an environment where diversity and uniqueness are celebrated is crucial. Surround your child with positive role models and share stories of successful individuals with autism to inspire them. Let them see that their potential is limitless and that their differences are a source of strength, not a barrier.

This journey of embracing and celebrating individuality is not just about benefiting your child. It enriches your entire family experience and deepens your understanding of what it means to be inclusive. By supporting your child's unique traits and celebrating their achievements, you're contributing to their overall well-being and helping them develop a strong, positive sense of self.

ABA At Home In Action:

Observe and Recognize Strengths

- Spend time observing your child to identify their interests, talents, and moments of joy and engagement.

- **Tip:** Keep a journal to note down these observations, highlighting specific instances where your child excels or shows enthusiasm.

2. Create a Supportive Environment for Exploration

- Provide your child with opportunities to explore a wide range of activities that align with their interests and strengths.

- **Tip:** Introduce activities gradually and ensure they are tailored to your child's preferences and abilities.

3. Provide Specific and Constructive Feedback

- Offer praise and constructive feedback that focuses on your child's efforts and accomplishments.

- **Tip:** Be specific in your praise, for example, "I love how you used different colors in your painting. It looks fantastic!"

4. Encourage Self-Expression

- Support your child in expressing themselves through creative outlets such as art, writing, music, or other activities they enjoy.

- **Tip:** Provide materials and a safe space for your child to engage in creative activities without judgment or pressure.

5. Promote Inclusivity and Advocacy

- Teach your child to advocate for themselves and their needs, ensuring they understand their unique strengths and rights.

- **Tip:** Role-play scenarios with your child to practice self-advocacy skills, and share stories of successful individuals with autism to inspire them.

I have had a lot of favorite moments working in what I do, but there are many moments that stand out—moments that remind me why I am so passionate about what I do. But nothing compares to the moment when I witness a child successfully implement the techniques we've taught them. It's in these moments that I see the real power of the work we do together.

I've had the privilege of watching children walk away from situations that once overwhelmed them, calmly taking deep breaths because they learned it helps them regain control. I've seen children, who once struggled with confidence, light up with pride as they tell themselves, "I DID IT," after accomplishing something they never thought possible.

These are not just victories for the children—they are victories for their parents as well.

One of the most rewarding experiences is seeing a mother or father look at their child with pure joy, witnessing a calmness where once there was a tantrum. These are the moments when parents realize that the strategies we've worked on together truly make a difference. The stress, the worry, the endless questions of, "Will this ever get better?" start to fade as they see their child thrive in ways they never imagined.

The work I do is more than just a job; it's a mission, a calling to help families find peace, understanding, and joy in the journey of raising a child with autism. My hope is that through this book, you will find the same sense of peace. I hope that the strategies, insights, and stories shared within these pages will empower you to guide your child toward their fullest potential.

As you implement the techniques I've outlined, I want you to remember that every small victory is a step forward. Every moment of progress, no matter how small, is a testament to your dedication and your child's incredible potential. This journey may have its challenges, but it is also filled with moments of triumph and joy.

Thank you for allowing me to be a part of your journey. It has been an honor to share in these moments with you, to witness your child's growth, and to support you in creating a future filled with hope and possibility.

May this book continue to guide you, inspire you, and bring you and your family the peace and happiness you deserve.

Unlock Extra Freebies and Connect with Me!

Thank you for your interest in Guiding Light: Navigating Autism with Empathy and Expertise! To show my appreciation, I'm excited to offer you some exclusive freebies designed to support you on your journey.

What's Included:

Printable Worksheets: Get practical, easy-to-use worksheets that help you implement the strategies from the book right at home.

Guided Checklists: Stay organized with checklists that simplify tasks like creating routines and tracking progress.

Exclusive Tips & Tricks: Receive additional insights and tips that didn't make it into the book, tailored to enhance your approach and understanding.

Go to **www.promptpathconsulting. com/resources** for additional freebies.

Want More Information?

I'm here to support you! If you have any questions, need further advice, or just want to connect, feel free to reach out. Here's how you can get in touch:

Email: kassandra@promptpathconsulting.com
Website: www.promptpathconsulting.com
Social Media: kassandraalvarez

Stay Connected!

Join my community to get the latest updates, share your experiences, and access even more resources designed to help you and your child thrive.

Thank you for being a part of this journey. I look forward to hearing from you and supporting you every step of the way!

Thank You For Reading My Book!

I really appreciate all of your feedback and
I love hearing what you have to say.

Please take two minutes now to leave a helpful review on
Amazon letting me know what you thought of the book
- Kassandra

www.ingramcontent.com/pod-product-compliance
Lightning Source LLC
Chambersburg PA
CBHW071524120626
46550CB00006B/2347